*Twayne's United States Authors Series*

*James Baldwin*

TUSAS 290

James Baldwin

# JAMES BALDWIN

## By LOUIS H. PRATT

*Florida Agricultural and*
*Mechanical University*

TWAYNE PUBLISHERS
A DIVISION OF G. K. HALL & CO., BOSTON

**Library of Congress Cataloging in Publication Data**

Pratt, Louis H
    James Baldwin.

    (Twayne's United States authors series  ;  TUSAS 290)
    Bibliography:    p. 147 - 54
    Includes index.
    1.   Baldwin, James, 1924 -          —Criticism and interpretation.
I.   Title.
PS3552.A45Z86        1978          818'.5'409          77-26001
ISBN 0-8057-7193-X

MANUFACTURED IN THE UNITED STATES OF AMERICA

For Karen and Kenneth as they dream new dreams, think new thoughts, and rise to new heights in pursuit of excellence.

# Contents

# About the Author

Louis H. Pratt is Associate Professor of English and Chairman of the Department of Languages and Literature at Florida A and M University, Tallahassee, Florida. He received the Bachelor of Science degree with honors from Savannah State College, the Master of Arts from Teachers College, Columbia University, and the Doctor of Philosophy degree from Florida State University.

A former public school teacher, Dr. Pratt has served as adjunct instructor of English at Savannah State College and instructor of English in the Thirteen College Curriculum Program at Florida A and M University. He is a recent contributor to the *College Language Association Journal*.

The present volume is a revision of Dr. Pratt's doctoral dissertation which was cited as "a major contribution to contemporary critical literature" and judged the best creative scholarship in American literature or folklore at Florida State University for 1974 - 75. In recognition of this achievement, Professor Pratt received the first annual J. Russell Reaver Award.

# Preface

Few black American writers have had a more profound impact on our culture than James Baldwin. Through his intensely personal art, Baldwin has achieved an extraordinary popular appeal which has made him one of the most widely read black writers in the twentieth century. The essay collection *Nobody Knows My Name* (1961) sold over two million copies, and the sale of a second collection, *The Fire Next Time* (1963), reached the million mark. The novel *Another Country* (1962), despite its generally unfavorable critical reception, sold four million copies. With the exception of Frank Yerby's novels, only one other book by a black writer made the bestseller list between 1895 and 1965: Richard Wright's autobiography, *Black Boy*, sold slightly over half a million copies in 1945.

It is unfortunate indeed that these writings have scarcely received the critical attention that they deserve. The majority of the magazine and newspaper criticism concerns the novels, the essays, or both; only brief, passing references are made to the short stories or the plays. Fern Eckman's biographical volume, *The Furious Passage of James Baldwin* (1966), now out of print, is a singular effort in that field.

In recognition of the compelling need for a more thorough assessment of Baldwin's writings, I have directed the focus of this book to the exploration of several of the virtually unexamined aspects of Baldwin's art. Because of the voluminous analyses of the collected essays, I have elected to treat them on a selective basis. Moreover, Baldwin's book reviews have been excluded, since they do not fall within the scope of this study. The emphasis in the first chapter is on Baldwin's artistic philosophy as it relates to his conception of a writer's "business" and the recurrent themes in his works. The second chapter is an analysis of the five short stories contained in *Going to Meet the Man* which seem to demonstrate most vividly Baldwin's ability to delve into the psychological states of his characters. A detailed treatment of style, theme, and technique in the novels is the concern of the third chapter. In the fourth chapter the plays are viewed against Baldwin's artistic philosophy, and attention is given to the common themes of illusion versus reality and the search for identity. The fifth chapter involves a discussion of representative essays both from aesthetic and social viewpoints, with an emphasis on the artistic achievement which they represent. The final chapter is a brief survey of critical opinion regarding the artistic stature that Baldwin has achieved in the modern American literary tradition.

My ultimate purpose has been a more precise delineation of the broader concerns with which Baldwin deals—issues which are drawn *not* in terms of the provincial problems of white versus black, but according to the universal concepts of freedom versus slavery, liberation versus oppression, reality versus illusion, identity versus darkness, confusion, and chaos.

Louis H. Pratt

*Florida Agricultural and Mechanical University*
*Tallahassee, Florida*

# Acknowledgments

Expressions of my profound gratitude are due the following persons who have been of invaluable assistance during the completion of this study:

To my wife, Darnell, my typist, chief sounding board, and layman-critic, who has been a paragon of patience and understanding under difficult and trying circumstances.

To Dr. Fred L. Standley of Florida State University for his wise counsel and unwavering support and encouragement.

To Mrs. Louise L. Owens and Dr. Luetta C. Milledge of Savannah State College and Dr. George E. Kent of the University of Chicago for their perceptive comments and suggestions.

To Mrs. Annette P. Thorpe of Florida A and M University for the invaluble advice which she offered during the initial stages of the manuscript.

To Dr. Therman B. O'Daniel and the *College Language Association Journal (CLAJ)* for permission to quote passages from O'Daniel's article, "James Baldwin: An Interpretive Study," which appeared in the September 1963 issue of *CLAJ*.

To Ms. Alice D. Phalen of G. K. Hall and Company for her cooperation in providing technical advice and suggestions.

To *Commentary* for granting permission to reprint quotations from James Baldwin's contribution to "Liberalism and the Negro: A Round Table Discussion," Copyright © 1964 by the American Jewish Committee, which appeared in the March 1964 issue of *Commentary*.

To Beacon Press for permission to quote from *Notes of a Native Son* by James Baldwin, Copyright © 1949, 1951, 1955 by James Baldwin.

To J. B. Lippincott and Company for permission to quote from *A Dialogue* by James Baldwin and Nikki Giovanni, Copyright © 1973 by James Baldwin and Niktom, Ltd. and *A Rap on Race* by Margaret Mead and James Baldwin, Copyright © 1971 by J. B. Lippincott Company.

To the Dial Press for permission to quote from the following

# Chronology

1924     James Arthur Baldwin born August 2 in New York City.

1930 -    Attended P.S. 24 and J.H.S. 139 (Frederick Douglass Junior
1938      High School). Composed lyrics of the farewell songs at
both schools. Published a short story, editorials, and
sketches in school newspaper, *The Douglass Pilot,* which he
edited. Studied under Countee Cullen, adviser to Douglass'
literary club.

1938     Began to preach at the Fireside Pentecostal Assembly.

1938 -    Attended De Witt Clinton High School. Published three
1942      stories with religious overtones in school newspaper, *The
Magpie:* "The Woman at the Well," "Mississippi Leg-
end," and "Incident in London." Shared the job of *Magpie*
editor-in-chief with classmate Richard Avedon.

1942     Renounced the ministry. Graduated from high school and
joined classmate, poet Emile Capouya, in Belle Mead, New
Jersey, as a railroad hand.

1944     Moved to Greenwich Village. Introduced to Richard
Wright by a mutual friend. Began to write first novel, *In
My Father's House.*

1945     Awarded Eugene Saxton Fellowship on the recommenda-
tion of Richard Wright.

1946     Launched professional career with a book review on Maxim
Gorki which appeared in *The Nation.* Wrote book reviews
for *The New Leader.*

1948     Received Rosenwald Fellowship. Published first essay,
"The Harlem Ghetto," and short story, "Previous Condition," in *Commentary.* Moved to Paris.

1953     *Go Tell It on the Mountain.*

1954     *The Amen Corner.* Awarded Guggenheim Fellowship.

1955     *Notes of a Native Son.* Edited *The Amen Corner* during its
Spring premiere performance at Howard University.

1956     *Giovanni's Room.* Received Partisan Review Fellowship
and the National Institute of Arts and Letters Award.

1957     Returned to the United States in July; visited the South for the first time and published his impressions in *Harper's* and *Partisan Review.*

1959    Awarded Ford Foundation Grant. Returned to Paris in November.

1960    Returned to United States in the Spring to write articles for *Esquire* and *Mademoiselle.* Travelled to Tallahassee, Florida in August to participate in CORE strategy session for student protests and sit-ins.

1961    *Nobody Knows My Name.* Best-selling essay collection won a certificate of recognition from the National Conference on Christians and Jews, and was selected by the Notable Books Council of the American Library Association as one of the outstanding books of the year. Departed for Europe.

1962    Best-selling novel, *Another Country.* Departed for Africa.

1963    Best-selling essay collection, *The Fire Next Time.* Received the George Polk Memorial Award for outstanding magazine reporting.

1964    Published *Blues for Mister Charlie* which opened at the ANTA Theater on Broadway on April 23 under the direction of Burgess Meredith. First professional production of *The Amen Corner* opened in Los Angeles under the direction of Frank Silvera. Published *Nothing Personal* (text by Baldwin, photographs by Richard Avedon).

1965    *Going to Meet the Man. The Amen Corner* opened on Broadway, and a second production toured Europe and the Near East. Appeared in a debate before 1200 students of the Cambridge Union Society at Cambridge University in support of the motion that "The American Dream is at the expense of the American Negro." Arguing against the proposition which carried overwhelmingly was *National Review* editor William F. Buckley, Jr.

1968    *The Amen Corner* and *Tell Me How Long the Train's Been Gone.*

1971    *A Rap on Race* (with Margaret Mead).

1972    *No Name in the Street* and *One Day, When I Was Lost.*

1973    *A Dialogue* (with Nikki Giovanni).

1974    Appeared on the Today Show with Barbara Walters in May to discuss new novel, *If Beale Street Could Talk.*

1976    *The Devil Finds Work.* Currently spends a great deal of his time in Istanbul and Paris and elsewhere on the European continent.

## CHAPTER 1

# "Common Experience, Uncommonly Probed"

I  *Exile and Return: An Artist in Search of Himself*

FERN Eckman describes the Harlem where James Arthur Baldwin was born as "geographically part of the United States but sociologically an island surrounded by the rest of the country."[1] In what seems a graphic elaboration on this statement, Baldwin himself recalls the terms on which the struggle for survival in the ghetto must depend: "The nature of the ghetto is somehow ultimately to make those skills which are immoral the only skills worth having. You haven't got to be sweet to survive in a ghetto; you've got to be cunning. You've got to make up the rules as you go along; there aren't any others. You can't call the cops."[2]

It was this environment that impressed upon the sensitive young Baldwin the crucial choice which he would ultimately be compelled to make: He must summon every available ounce of stamina and courage to escape the sordid world of pimps, junkies, prostitutes, racketeers, and con men; or he must abandon his search for identity, surrender himself, and become engulfed by the vicious circumstances of his surroundings.

In a very real sense, Baldwin's escape takes place on two levels: the personal and the artistic. There was the grim, religious fanaticism of a stepfather, an evangelical preacher, who hated the bastard son born to his wife prior to their marriage. And there was the elder Baldwin's repressive dominance of a submissive wife and children, set against the environmental abyss of liquor, drugs, sex, and crime. On the artistic level, Baldwin felt that he could not survive the institution of segregation in this country which reduced him to "merely a Negro writer." He wanted to discover how the uniqueness of his experience might be used to establish a common bond among humanity.

It was this quest that spurred Baldwin into a hastily arranged, self-imposed exile to Paris on November 11, 1948. The next nine years were spent among a literary coterie of established writers which included Chester Himes, James Jones, Philip Roth, William Styron, Norman Mailer, and Richard Wright. During these years the young Baldwin began to formulate his artistic credo, and he began to write. His first novel, *Go Tell It on the Mountain*, appeared in 1953, followed by a book of essays, *Notes of a Native Son*, in 1955. The following year a second novel, *Giovanni's Room*, was published. Undergirded by these achievements, Baldwin returned to the United States in July, 1957.

Interestingly enough, the return to native soil was motivated by a keen sensitivity to the embryonic black civil rights struggle which had begun on the frontiers of an indifferent America. That fall Baldwin crossed the Mason-Dixon line for an initial, first-hand assessment of the racial situation in Atlanta, Charlotte, Birmingham, and other parts of the "Deep South." It was his effort to understand, to fathom the Southern situation which, he discovered, differed from the Northern predicament only in that Southerners employed a different strategy to meet a common objective: keeping the black man "in his place."

As the storm of social change began to lash and whip the shores of America in the 1960s, so the literary winds began to shift their course, signalling the emergence of Imamu Amiri Baraka (LeRoi Jones) as the chief exponent of the Black Arts Movement. Jones and his circle of writers issued the call for artists who would proudly accept the term "black writer" and actively seek to create an aesthetic based on the idea of "a black man talking to other black men, not talking simply to an audience of middle-class, credit-card-carrying whites."[3] Baldwin, however, refused to align himself with this new artistic stance. Choosing to abide by his earlier decision, he continued to insist upon recognition as an "American writer," bound only by the need, the obligation, to practice his craft.

In exercising this prerogative, James Baldwin has found himself at odds with current white literary trends as well. He contends that mainstream art is directed toward a complacent and apathetic audience, and it is designed to confirm and reinforce that sense of well-being. It functions, ultimately, to imprison us within the shell of our illusions: "Most contemporary fiction, like most contemporary theater, is designed to corroborate your fantasies and make you walk out whistling. I don't want you to whistle at *my* stuff, baby. I want you to be sitting on the edge of your chair waiting for nurses to carry you out.''[4]

Baldwin's writings are, then, by their very nature, iconoclastic. While Black Arts focuses on a black-oriented artistry, Baldwin is concerned with the destruction of the fantasies and delusions of a contented audience which is determined to avoid reality. In his review of *Going to Meet the Man,* Seymour Krim assesses Baldwin's "chief strength" as his unusual adeptness with the "common experience uncommonly probed": "He has almost always tried to dig into the humbling soil of the experience of the Negro, the expatriate, the homosexual, and come out with uneasy, disturbing truths. . . ."[5] Indeed it is this sensitivity, this perceptiveness which lies at the heart of Baldwin's artistic appeal.

## II  *Sifting the Ashes, Probing the Past*

It seems an incontestable fact that any discussion of literary art must begin with an attempt to define those artistic assumptions which undergird that art. Unless we can come to grips with these foundations, unless we are able to align ourselves with the author's purpose, we run the risk of misunderstanding the specific impact that the artistry was intended to convey. Consequently, we can venture into a consideration of James Baldwin's artistry only after we have examined the underpinnings of the unsettling "truths" which he presents to us.

The first of these assumptions is that an artist is produced by his society, and the people—the masses—are the source of his inspiration, the wellspring of his creativity. He does not *decide* upon his calling; he *discovers* the artistic mantle upon his shoulders, and he rises to accept it: "What you do, you do because you must. The way fish breathe water, writers write; if they don't, they'll die."[6]

In 1955 Baldwin listed his sources as ". . . the King James Bible, the rhetoric of the store-front church, something ironic and violent and perpetually understated in Negro speech—and something of Dickens' love of bravura— . . ."[7] but he has since retreated from the esoteric implications of this claim. Eleven years later, at a conference on "The Negro Writer's Vision of America," a reassessment of this position produced a totally different response: "My models—my private models—are not Hemingway, not Faulkner, not Dos Passos, or indeed any American writer. I model myself on jazz musicians, dancers, a couple of whores and a few junkies. . . ."[8] Inherent in this statement is an acknowledgment of the grass roots origins, a recognition of the blood, sweat, pain, suffering, and tears of the past, and an awareness that the writer must tap that source if he is to survive.

A second assumption that pervades Baldwin's writings is that of exploitation of experience. The artist draws not only upon his positive experiences, but upon the negative ones as well. Consequently, as a prerequisite to becoming a great writer, he must recognize and accept his past, however painful that acceptance might be. He must gather the courage to sift the ashes of his frustrations, nightmares, and inhibitions in order to salvage the essence of these experiences if he is to fulfill his role. And he must analyze his joys and jubilations in order to extract their significance: "The only way to [be a great writer], it seems to me, is not to complain about anything that happens to you, but to *use* whatever happens to you—from starvation to champagne. . . ."[9]

It is significant that Baldwin was never able to capitalize upon his experience until he fled the United States. In the atmosphere of the French capital, as he recalls in "The Discovery of What It Means To Be an American," he became liberated from the need to justify his existence. The immensity of this freedom, filtered through the blues of Bessie Smith, enabled Baldwin to reestablish contact with his past, his deeply buried experiences. It was this reconciliation which provided the challenge for the exploration of those experiences and for the emergence of James Baldwin the writer. This had not been possible in America because he had attempted to suppress those experiences: " . . . for years I would not touch watermelon. . . ."[10] In Paris he learned to channel and use the totality of his experiences in the production of his art. Attendant to this discovery was the realization that the artist cannot exist apart from the society that produced him. Thus he returned to America out of the necessity for reuniting himself with his past.

The concept of the writer as prophet is the third assumption which is revealed in Baldwin's writings. The artist functions as a social corrective; he alone is capable of helping us to reconcile our exalted images of ourselves with the truth about us. It is this truth which we actively seek to avoid because the terror of our deeds is too great for us to confront. The artist, then, becomes the "yeast" which upsets our tendency toward indifference and paves the way for a reconciliation between these two divergences: "This ferment, this disturbance, is the responsibility, and the necessity, of writers. It is, alas, the truth that to be an American writer today means mounting an unending attack on all that Americans believe themselves to hold sacred. It means fighting an astute and agile guerrilla warfare with that American complacency which so inadequately masks the American panic."[11]

Thus, the writer is engaged in a perpetual battle to overrule our objections and continue his probe into the very depths of our past. His constant concern is the catastrophic failure of the American Dream and the devastating inability of the American people to deal with that calamity. He must ponder this failure and drive to the heart of the tragedy. He must help us to realize that unless we are able to come to terms with reality, we can never be free. We shall remain forever isolated from human communication and intercourse, unable to achieve and maintain our identity: "We are very cruelly trapped between what we would like to be and what we actually are, and we cannot possibly become what we would like to be until we are willing to ask ourselves just why the lives we lead on this continent are so empty, so tame and so ugly. . . ."[12] And because we are trapped between self-imposed image and reality, we are unable to release our full energies in the identity quest. We are prisoners of the "undiscovered self."

The paradox here is that the artist is *of* the people, a *part* of the people, and yet he is alone. Isolation, a condition which the people must avoid, is a circumstance that the writer must accept. Isolation becomes a necessary wedge between the writer and his society, but he can never allow his contact with that society to become severed. Though a product of the people, he must nevertheless maintain a certain remoteness from his society in order to cultivate the position of objectivity which is indispensable to the prophetic role of the artist. This brings us to the fourth assumption, the "division of labor":

There is a division of labor in the world—as I see it—and the people have quite enough reality to bear, simply getting through their lives, raising their children, dealing with the external conundrums of birth, taxes, and death. They do not do this with all the wisdom, foresight, or charity one might wish; nevertheless, this is what they are always doing and it is what the writer is always describing. There is nothing else to describe. This effort at description is itself extraordinarily arduous, and those who are driven to make this effort are by virtue of this fact somewhat removed from the people.[13]

On the one side we have the drawers of water and the hewers of wood; on the other stand the artists, those rare individuals who actually *see* us in our yearnings and strivings and who are able to illuminate the darkness in our progress toward the discovery of self.

Many critics have searched Baldwin's writings for "solutions" to the problems which he presents in his indictments of society. This has proved to be a futile endeavor because the division of responsibility requires that the illuminators and the reformers inhabit different spheres. Consequently, the artist is not responsible for curing our social ills; he is concerned with the task of revelation: "He has to tell, because nobody else in the world *can* tell what it is like to be alive. All I've ever wanted to do is tell that. I'm not trying to solve anybody's problems, not even my own. I'm just trying to outline what the problems are."[14] Baldwin's position here is analogous to that of Henrik Ibsen, who, when frequently questioned about solutions to the problems posed in his dramas, steadfastly maintained that his province was solely within the realm of significant questions; his concern was not with the answers to those questions. Like Ibsen, Baldwin is always wary of aligning himself with moral codes and political causes. His business is to observe, to analyze, to question: "How have we managed to become what we have, in fact, become? And if we are, as, indeed, we seem to be, so empty and so desperate, what are we to do about it? How shall we put ourselves in touch with reality? How is an American to become a man; . . . how is America to become a nation?"[15] The people are responsible for taking these questions to heart and endeavoring to effect satisfactory solutions.

In Baldwin's canon, the artist must confine his attention to the prophetic mode; he must never attempt to find answers to the questions which he has posed because this exceeds the boundaries of his concern. This "division of labor" concept is reflected in Baldwin's reaction to Norman Mailer's proposed candidacy for the mayoralty of New York:

You're one of the very few writers around who might really become a great writer, who might help to excavate the buried consciousness of this country, and you want to settle for being the lousy mayor of New York. *It's not your job.* . . . I do not feel that a writer's responsibility can be discharged in this way. I do not think, if one is a writer, that one escapes it by trying to become something else. One does *not* become something else. One becomes nothing. . . .[16]

The final and most pervasive assumption found in Baldwin's art is that all of mankind is united by virtue of their humanity. Consequently, the ultimate purpose of the writer, from Baldwin's perspective, is to discover that sphere of commonality where, although differences exist, those dissimilarities are stripped of their power to block communication and stifle human intercourse. It is this common ground that we have been simultaneously seeking and avoiding for many generations:

When I am writing a novel, I am writing about me and all of you, and the great difficulty is to discover what connects us. Something connects us, and what it is is hidden. It is not science or prosperity; it is not to be found in any church, so far as I know— . . . Whatever is going to unite us from here on cannot be what has united us until now. Some other basis will have to be established if we are all going to remain alive, human, free.[17]

It is this connecting power that Baldwin holds out to us as the only hope for Western civilization. Having lost faith in the practice of Christianity, he continues to cling to the theoretical basis of morality upon which Christianity was founded: love. Having failed to find this power within the Christian church, Baldwin has renounced his ministry to seek it in the world among his fellowmen. The object of his quest, the love in which he continues to believe, is an active, positive force with the potential to effect a transformation in the lives of men; it is ". . . something more like fire, like the wind, something which can change you. I mean energy. I mean a passionate belief, a passionate knowledge of what a human being can do, and become, what a human being can do to change the world in which he finds himself."[18]

But the implications of love are vast indeed. Loving means removing the mask, exposing our psyches to the stark, cold reality which has long been buried in the vault of our subconscious. This is the great threat to our security which we seem determined at all costs to avoid. And because we can never attain selfhood in isolation from humanity, we must be willing to pay the price, unmask our illusions and inhibitions, and face the terrors of these revelations.

## III *Transforming the Rage: Protest, Prefiguration, and Separatism*

Prior to Baldwin's entry upon the literary scene, the dominant trend among black artists was protest literature, and the hero was Richard Wright. Wright viewed the process of artistic creation as a safety valve for releasing the rage and fear which grew inevitably out of the black American experience, and he pursued *Native Son* as an "experiment," an opportunity ". . . to free myself of this burden of impressions and feeling, recast them into the image of Bigger, and make him true."[19] Wright tells us, further, that the creation of a "true" Bigger necessarily involved an attempt. ". . . to objectify in words some insight derived from my living in the form of action, scene, and dialogue."[20] Consequently, Wright's efforts seem to be directed toward the fictional but realistic presentation of his rage.

While Baldwin accepted the cathartic function of literature, he saw a basic inadequacy inherent in Wright's artistic theory. Although Baldwin identified with the rage which Wright felt, he contended that the artist must go beyond the mere depiction of that rage. He must be able to analyze that fury before it can be transformed into an identifiable human experience. Therefore, Baldwin was appalled by Wright's conversion of raw, unmitigated rage into violence in the pages of his fiction: ". . . violence, as in so much of Wright's work is gratuitous and compulsive. . . . The violence is gratuitous and compulsive because the root of the violence is never examined. The root is rage."[21]

Essentially, this is the *faux pas*, Baldwin argues, which damns Richard Wright, denies his novels elevation to the high dominion of literary artistry, and simultaneously consigns them to the bleak world of social protest and racism. This failure, Baldwin contends, results from Wright's inability to distinguish between his social and artistic roles; hence his tendency to convert his experience into protest and propaganda. One of the most recent theories on the Wright-Baldwin controversy has been advanced by Kichung Kim, who argues that the artistic gap arises from the different concepts of man held by the two writers. Wright views man solely against the background of reality: what he has been and what he is. For Baldwin, however, this concept is not comprehensive enough. Therefore, Kim contends that the shortcoming which Baldwin finds in the works of Wright and other protest novelists, is not so much that they had failed to give a faithful account of the actual conditions of man but rather that they had failed to be steadfast in their devotion . . .to what man might and ought to be. Such a man . . . will not only survive oppression but will be strengthened by it.[22]

Baldwin sought to probe and penetrate the roots of protest literature—the anger and the rage—in order to discover a recognizable human emotion which reflected not only the reality but the potentiality of man. Thus was born a prefigurative literature which emerged not as docile appeal, but as the warning of an imminent revolution with coexistence as its objective: "The terms of our revolution—the *American* revolution—are these: not that I drive you out or that you drive me out, but that we learn to live together."[23]

A third trend, the Black Arts movement, rejects the literature of protest and its implicit assumption that redress of grievances can be accomplished. Similarly, it condemns the literature of prefiguration on the grounds that warnings have no efficacy and that coexistence is no longer possible or desirable. Out of these denials has evolved a basic concept which characterizes the Black Arts involvement: the inseparable union of the black artist with the black audience. It follows, then, that Amiri Baraka's (Le Roi Jones) view of the warfare to which Baldwin refers is radically different. For him revolution becomes "warfare between that which generates and signifies life and that which is death. . . . The death-battle raging around and through us [is] an actual death struggle between two cultures."[24]

White culture and the white aesthetic as well is a sterile, stagnated structure, equally incapable of rejuvenating itself as it is of providing for the expression of black artists. For Baraka there can be no common ground; there can be no compromise. The death of the white culture gives rise to the black aesthetic as a living, viable alternative, free from the domination of the white power structure. Not only are his plays directed exclusively toward a black audience, but Baraka resolutely contends that these dramas have no message whatsoever for white people.

On the other hand, the question of audience, for Baldwin, is a complex consideration. The black audience becomes a powerful entity, in need of discovering and coming to grips with its past as well as utilizing that history as a bridge to the vast and unlimited expanses of selfhood. Baldwin exhorts whites to summon the courage to face their "ghastly deeds" and realize that we will make the revolution together or not at all. Thus, he rejects the term "black writer" as embraced by the Black Arts Movement, preferring to consider himself a "writer," pure and simple. As such, then, his artistic mission is to shake up whites and wake up blacks.

Inherent in the Black Arts philosophy is the concept of two Americas, one white and one black, the divergent cultures of which, by their very history and nature, preclude reconciliation. The black man, as an element of Western society, "remains an integral part of that society, but irrevocably outside of it, a figure like Melville's Bartleby. He is an American, capable of identifying emotionally with this society, but he is also, forever, outside that culture, an observer."[25] Recognition of the black man as an outsider demands the creation of new institutions which will be culturally and financially independent of white domination. It demands the creation of a new literature designed to accomplish the liberation of black people.

This practical objective of liberation has led Baraka to oppose Baldwin's concept of division of responsibility in society. For Baraka the black artist is both *of* and *in* the community to which he owes his existence. He is neither isolated nor alienated from that community. Therefore, Baraka shuns the role of interrogator and seeks to provide some of the crucial answers to the social and cultural needs of black people: "We need plays to be dealing with Urban Renewal and plays to be solving the problems of the community, or offering solutions, and not plays that are always talking from some kind of liberal "artistic" vantage point that do not take any stand on anything. The playwright is not supposed to be the invisible man."[26] Baraka thus issues the call for the artist as a man of action as opposed to the man of thought.

Until recently black literature has been structured on white "bourgeois idealistic projections," Baraka argues in "The Myth of a 'Negro Literature,' " and black writers have heretofore concerned themselves with "striving for respectability." Brushing aside the writings of Jean Toomer, Richard Wright, Ralph Ellison, and Baldwin, he concludes that a legitimate black literature does not exist. This is a rather questionable judgment, as Cecil Brown points out, because inherent in the abnegation of a literature is the denial of the people who produced that art: "A literature of a people is not something whose existence is dependent on somebody's definitions; it exists if the people exist; if there is a people, there is a literature.

A people can have a magnificent literature, a frivolous literature, a supernatural literature, but they can not *not* have a literature, for a people's literature is nothing more than their own repertory of myths, myths being the manner in which they decide to organize their experience in and about nature."[27] What Baraka's movement represents, then, is a trend in the development of black literature, not the beginning of that literature, as he would have us believe.

Perhaps the greatest dichotomy between the artistic philosophies of Baldwin and Baraka concerns the issue of love versus hate. Baraka contends that hatred of whites is the natural and inevitable result of the experience of being black in America. He condones the hostility of blacks on the grounds that, in spite of the masks worn by black people in this country for centuries, hatred is the only reasonable reaction to oppression and subjugation. Baldwin, however, had been forced into a confrontation with his bitterness toward whites early in his search for identity. And he had discovered that hatred has the power to destroy. Hatred has no perpetrators, only victims. This recognition has given rise to his vision of the redemptive role of blacks in American society, as Hoyt Fuller suggests: "He [Baldwin] feels that the Negro masses, by virtue of their long and forced exclusion from the so-called 'mainstream of American life,' alone have retained a vision of a society constructed on the principles of justice and equality."[28] This seems to explain why Baldwin is committed to the task of exhortation. Blacks alone, like Grandma in Edward Albee's *The American Dream*, have, in a sense, become a repository of that dream; it is they who must preserve that vision, those standards of moral and spiritual value, if ever we are to achieve coexistence, if ultimately we are to survive. Through love, and only through love will this redemption become possible.

## IV  *A Bridging of the Gap*

In considering these differences between Baldwin's artistic philosophy and that of Black Arts, we must not lose sight of "that rare common ground" of agreement. In *The Fire Next Time*, Baldwin recalls his youthful ministry and delivers a scathing attack on the Christian church which, ironically, suggests a departure from the artist-as-interrogator concept to the community-action position maintained by Baraka: ". . . when I faced a congregation, it began to take all the strength I had not to stammer, not to curse, not to tell them to throw away their Bibles and get off their knees and go home and organize, for example, a rent strike. . . . There was no love in the church. It was a mask for hatred and self-hatred and despair. . . ."[29]

Basically, this is the attitude toward Christianity that is expressed by the supporters of the Black Arts Movement. Christianity becomes a white man's religion, devoid of all love and compassion, designed to justify the social, political, and economic subjugation of the black man. The result of this influence, they contend, was the devastating assumption that endurance of the pains, the sufferings, the humiliations, and the frustrations inflicted by white society was a necessary prerequisite to the joy and happiness of the afterlife. Closely aligned with the Black Muslim theology, Black Arts rejects the *totality* of the Christian frame of reference. The white man becomes the "devil" whom they hate, and the concept of love, which has no practical influence in the lives of white Christians, is also repudiated.

In abandoning Christianity, however, Baldwin never rejects the possibilities afforded by the transforming power of love. It is essential, he argues, to renounce the Christian church as the source of lovelessness and hypocrisy, but never does he counsel hatred. The failure of the church "to make us larger, freer, and more loving"[30] resulted from the perversion of the concept of love. Consequently, Baldwin has rejected the church as the source of that perversion, and he has endeavored to preach love as a "touchstone" and guiding influence in our lives among his fellowmen outside of the church. He is not an orthodox Christian believer in any sense of the term, but, unlike the Black Arts exponents, he retains an infinite, abiding faith in the power of love in human affairs.

A second issue on which there is partial agreement is the function of existing art. In contrasting "Show Biz" with Black Theater, Baraka reflects Baldwin's concern that current art merely serves to "corroborate" our fantasies: "Black Theater should be providing consciousness. Show Biz does not do anything to raise the level of consciousness. It does quite the contrary; it is antithetical to consciousness. . . ."[31] It is this "consciousness" which Baldwin also feels is vital to his art, which serves to heighten an awareness among blacks, rather than confirm their apathy and complacency. The ideological split comes, however, on the question of audience. For Baraka, it is both impossible and unnecessary to disturb the white establishment; his singular preoccupation is with black people.

Baldwin approaches the same goal by directing his work toward both black and white audiences.

Although Amiri Baraka is the dominant influence in the Black Arts Movement, other artists working within this school have views which tend to reflect a synthesis of the Baldwin and Baraka philosophies. Among these artists is playwright Douglas Turner Ward. On the crucial question of audience, for example, Ward seems to have reached a compromise between the two positions: "The screaming need is for a sufficient audience of *other Negroes,* better informed through commonly shared experience to readily understand debate, confirm, or reject the truth or falsity of his creative explorations. Not necessarily an all-black audience to the exclusion of whites but, for the playwright, certainly his primary audience, the first persons of his address, potentially the most advanced, the most responsive or most critical. . . ."[32]

On another central principle, separatism, Ward's position closely resembles Baldwin's. Black expression, he maintains, may be accomplished within the existing artistic structure as well as outside of it; isolation is not an inevitability. The key factor, he contends, is that the artist maintain absolute integrity as he pursues his talent; "He should be free and flexible to pursue whatever avenue is available to his development. But wherever he is, his black commitment cannot be threatened if he retains autonomy over the specifics of his artistic and personal participation."[33] This artistic philosophy allows for the inclusion of whites in the playwright's audience, the participation of whites in the production of black art, and the freedom of the black artist to capitalize upon all avenues for the expression of his art.

### V    *Shifting Sands: A Question of Viability*

Perhaps the most significant question at hand now concerns the direction in which Baldwin's artistic sensibilities will lead him in his future writings. Toward the end of the 1960's it appeared that Baldwin was moving closer to the artistic philosophy of the Black Arts Movement. In 1969, for example, his candid response to the question, "Can Black and White Artists Still Work Together?" indicated that he was on the verge of abandoning his prefigurative posture. He had apparently concluded that warnings and exhortations no longer served any useful purpose: "I will state flatly that the bulk of this country's white population impresses me, and has so impressed me for a very long time, as being beyond any conceivable hope of moral rehabilitation. They have been white, if I may so put it, too long; they have been married to the lie of white supremacy too long."[34]

Indeed this is a turning point for Baldwin. The tone here is clearly one of hopelessness; it is far removed from the optimistic attitude that characterized his writings earlier in the decade. It stands in sharp contrast to the coexistence which he calls the "terms" of the current "American Revolution." The ideological drift is toward the Black Arts concept of an irreconcilable duality in American society. Baldwin seems driven by this premise to the conclusion that artistic coexistence is not possible because " . . . the system under which black and white artists in this country work is geared to the needs of a people who, so far from being able to abandon the doctrine of white supremacy, seem prepared to blow up the globe to maintain it."[35]

Ironically enough, the progression of the mid-1970's has brought Baldwin full circle. The frustration and the futility expressed in his writings at the turn of the decade have given way to a message of hope. On May 19, 1976 Baldwin stood before an audience at Morehouse College in Atlanta, Georgia to receive an honorary doctor of letters. In these remarks he struck an unmistakable note of confident optimism which bordered on exuberance:

> When I was born, blacks generally were born trapped into a white man's fantasy. Black children are not trapped into a white man's fantasy now. . . . I feel a great wheel turning. This has never been a white country and the truth is coming out. Blacks have always been a part of this country but the country was never able to accept that. But we are flesh of the flesh, bone of the bone. And we will triumph.[36]

It was a celebration, an expression of faith in the possibility of restructuring the institutions of our society so that our children can not only survive but flourish as well.

One of the themes which Baldwin has echoed again and again is that we must save America for our children. Posterity, then, becomes the cornerstone of our salvation. In a magazine article which appeared in June, 1976, Baldwin begins his informal talk with the women in the prison facility at Riker's Island with this same reaffirmation of faith in the possibility of black survival in America: "We all have to find out how to deal with and change the position we're in. The most important thing for me is how to save our children."[37] It is this idea which forms the framework for *If Beale Street Could Talk* as Tish, Ernestine, Frank, Sharon, and Joe combine their talents and meager resources to rescue Fonny's unborn offspring from those sinister forces of our society which are determined to accomplish his destruction. And again in *The Devil Finds Work*, we find Baldwin at work on this theme:

Every trial, every beating, every drop of blood, every tear, were meant to be used by us for a day that was coming—for a day that was certainly coming: not for us, perhaps, but for our children.[38]

Our generation, he argues, has been concerned with survival. And our success has paved the way not for our own transcendence, but for the triumph of our children. This provides the inspiration for Baldwin in his work, and, simultaneously, it becomes the motivating idea for our renewed courage and vigor in the midst of the struggle.

It is difficult indeed to predict whether or not the optimism of the 1970's will continue to prevail in Baldwin's writings. Yet, he does seem to have a continuing commitment to the role of "disturber of the peace," and this suggests that at least a guarded optimism will prevail in his writings in the future.

In presenting these divergent artistic opinions, my purpose has not been to declare James Baldwin "the leading black writer," and I have resisted the conclusion that the Black Arts Movement "is now the dominant trend among black writers." Such epithets, aside from their hollow superficiality, follow the trend in white criticism of labeling and grouping black writers in order to " . . . limit severely the expansion of the talents of Negro writers and confine them to a literary ghetto from which only one Negro name at a time may emerge. . . ."[39] Rather, the design has been the consideration of these philosophies as evidence of the unprecedented, autonomous vitality that black art has achieved in late twentieth-century America.

All too often blacks have been misguided in their efforts to assert the ideological superiority of one trend over the other. In far too many instances, black critics have been prone to extol the virtues of one writer by condemning another writer as being "not black enough." It is this self-defeating, internal warfare which serves no constructive end and which, ultimately, brings chaos and destruction.

We must begin to realize that the viability of the entire spectrum of art by black Americans, like that of any other artistic tradition, is entirely dependent upon the  extent to which it is able to accommodate its diverse elements. Within this scheme of things, there seems to be little evidence that Baldwin's art has lost its power. The myth of "*the* black writer" has been perpetuated by those whites who maintain the "literary ghetto" and by those blacks who, compelled by the need to find their niche, have taken up residence in that ghetto under the calculated delusion that they must fight their way to the top.

CHAPTER 2

# The Fear and the Fury

I *Artist, Prophet, and Revelator*

PERHAPS the most basic assumption underlying Baldwin's artistic philosophy is the concept of writer as prophet. The creative artist, Baldwin contends, is endowed with an extraordinary spiritual and moral insight which reveals the most disturbing truths about ourselves and gives rise to his role as social visionary. Thus, the writer is *compelled* to face the truth about himself, shatter our personal fantasies, illusions, and myths, and reveal the excruciating, unsettling truths about us and our society.

The title of the collection of short stories, *Going to Meet the Man*, is especially illustrative of Baldwin in his role as revelator. Here he is concerned with the frustrating, depressing, and intolerable conditions of urban life and society and their explosive impact on the black man in twentieth-century America. As a writer at war with his society, he deals "with the gutter and the grime, the impersonality and the anonymity, the isolation and the confinement of the sprawling modern metropolis, with all of its conflict and complexity, its teeming thousands of population, its concrete and steel—and especially the impact upon those within the lower socioeconomic stratum."[1] These stories attempt to probe directly into the essence of the black experience in the United States and to expose the myths and the realities which lie at the root of that experience. On a broader level the stories can be viewed as human efforts to come to grips with the issue of man's existence and survival amid the daily crucialities of life.

The crises presented in this collection call attention to the need for a clear perception and a genuine understanding of the deepest, most intimate needs of humanity caught in the overwhelming, ultimate struggle of life and death. This discussion of *Going to Meet the Man* will focus on five categories of cruciality, based on the

31

seven situations as identified by Carl Michalson: (1) origin and destiny—man's efforts to analyze the origin, the meaning, and the goal of life; (2) anxiety—man's efforts to cope with the inner conflicts arising from his efforts to find answers to the questions of origin and destiny; (3) doubt—the threat of meaninglessness which prompts man to question the significance of life; (4) frustration—man's unsuccessful efforts to determine the meaning of his suffering in order to determine the meaning of life; (5) guilt—man's vague sense of unworthiness, of failure—not for something he has done, but for something for which he feels the need for atonement.[2] The sole relief from these experiences can come only through truth as an illuminating and liberating catalyst which gives rise to an understanding of one's origins and destiny.

## II   *White Image, Black Image*

The life of the black man in America today is replete with crucial crises on a day-to-day basis. His very existence is threatened by the inner conflict between the satisfaction of his basic needs and the nameless, paralyzing, and insurmountable fears—conscious and unconscious—which grow out of the experience of being black in a white-oriented society. These fears result in the imploding of the personality and render him incapable of coping effectively with the situations of life. In turn, the implosion gives rise to explosion, the sudden release of black fury from which white society has sought to cushion itself through the most brutal and savage means possible. It is this fear and this fury that Baldwin explores in *Going to Meet the Man*.[3]

In "Sonny's Blues," for example, we encounter the first-person narrator, Sonny's brother, who is comfortably surrounded by the trappings of middle-class success. He has escaped "the vivid, killing streets" of Harlem, obtained a college education and a high school teaching job, and he has become firmly entrenched in middle-class traditions. Yet there is a sense of uneasiness as he stares at the newspaper announcing Sonny's arrest and observes " . . . my own face, trapped in the darkness which roared outside." (86) He has yet to become aware of the enslaving darkness within himself.

Unaware of his origin and destiny—his identity—the narrator has fabricated an image of himself, and he has tried desperately to fashion his life in accordance with that image. He now lives with his family in a rundown apartment house and attempts to maintain the facade of middle-class respectability. He is now a "collaborator," an "accomplice" of his oppressors because, as Baldwin points out, "they think it's important to be white, and you think it's important to be white; they think it's a shame to be black and you think it's a shame to be black. And you have no corroboration around you of any other sense of life. All the corroboration around you is in terms of the white majority standards. . . ."[4]

In a state of complacency, the narrator manages to sustain the charade until the news of Sonny's arrest begins to intrude upon his delusions. Although he had been "suspicious" about his brother's possible involvement with drugs, he could not reach out to help the boy. There was no way to reconcile Sonny's drug addiction with the white image which he had accepted for himself: "I couldn't find any room for it anywhere inside me. I had kept it outside me for a long time. I hadn't wanted to know . . ." (87). Similarly, the narrator's adherence to white standards rendered him unable to understand Sonny's preference for jazz over classical music: "I simply couldn't see why on earth he'd want to spend his time hanging around nightclubs, clowning around on bandstands, while people pushed each other around on a dance floor. It seemed—beneath him, somehow . . ." (103).

In spite of these efforts, the narrator is unable to repress an inner anxiety resulting from the compulsive urge to discover his identity. He is deeply affected by the reminiscences of Sonny, the conversation with the talkative boy, and the encounter with the barmaid dancing to a "black and bouncy" tune. All of this begins to impinge upon his fabricated reality, and he discovers a powerful impulse to avoid the confrontation and to preserve his cherished illusion. Yet, in spite of himself, he begins to realize the need for "seeking . . . that part of ourselves which had been left behind" (95).

For the older brother, Sonny becomes a living embodiment of his identity and heritage, and it dawns upon the narrator's consciousness that he must find a way to open a line of communication with that past. But in the Baldwin canon, this channel can be opened only through personal suffering. Thus, the untimely death of the narrator's little girl Grace serves as a bridge to Sonny's anguish and experience and reunites the brothers.

At this point, Sonny's remarkable insight into the nature of suffering as an unavoidable aspect of daily life becomes apparent: "There's no way of getting it out—that storm inside. You can't talk it and you can't make love with it, and when you finally try to get with it and play it, you realize *nobody's* listening. So *you've* got to listen. You got to find a way to listen" (115). It is this perception, this sense of frustration, that characterizes the younger brother's superior wisdom. As the older brother listens to "Am I Blue?" he grows in the knowledge that the story of human suffering, which is as old as recorded time, must continue to be sung and listened to, because it alone can shed a ray of light on the massive darkness in our lives. It was here, in Sonny's "world," in Sonny's "kingdom," that a full awareness dawned: "I understood, at last that he could help us to be free if we would listen, that he would never be free until we did" (122). Thus, Sonny's brother has become liberated from the enslaving image of himself projected by white society. He has recovered a personal history and an ethnic pride, excavated from the ruins of his warped personality. He is now free to discover his own destiny. Sonny the teacher, by virtue of his experiences, becomes Sonny the elder, by virtue of his wisdom. Once the narrator draws near to listen, the blues becomes the means by which Sonny is able to lead his brother, through a confrontation with the meaning of life, into a discovery of self.

### III   *Implosion, Explosion: Fragmentation of the Psyche*

Typically, the black experience in America can best be described in a single word: accommodation. Either the black man must accept and reinforce the image of himself that white society holds before him and complacently adapt himself to white standards, or he must become actively engaged in a perpetual struggle to discover his own origins, define his own image, and refute the overwhelming, inescapable myths and illusions upon which the very structure of our society has been built. Daily he must fight the battle, or he must risk losing the war.

It is this ambivalence, this dichotomy, that Baldwin describes in the statement, "  . . .  no American Negro exists who does not have his private Bigger Thomas living in the skull . . .",[5] for each of these falsifications has its roots in fear. Sometimes this fear leads to an acceptance of the *status quo* (as in the case of Sonny's brother); at other times, it gives rise to implosion, the inner frustration and the eventual explosive fury resulting from this constant conflict with society. It is the latter situation that Baldwin depicts in "Previous Condition."

The motif of fear is introduced early in the story. Peter has nocturnal nightmares in which he is constantly running; he awakens trembling, cold, and wet with sweat. He never remembers *why* he is running or what his dreams are about; he only knows that they started a long time ago. He goes to sleep frightened, and he awakens terrified, to face another day of nightmares. Jobless and broke, he lives a miserable life in "the kind of room that defeated you" (69). Assuming the role of a fugitive, he leaves after everybody else has left, returns when the other tenants are asleep, and lives in constant fear that his jealously guarded secret will be discovered: He is a black man living in a rooming house in a white neighborhood.

These are the brief facts of Peter's existence, confirmed by Peter himself: "You get so used to being hit you find you're always waiting for it" (78). This is a typical experience shared by blacks in America, who, in order to survive a hostile, racist society, "have acquired such habits of inferiority and have evolved such a way of life . . . that they have become in some sense accustomed to their oppression. I don't mean that they accept it or that they like it, but they *know* it. *They know it.* They do not call the cops as other American citizens do; they don't have the same expectations."[6] Peter's habits of inferiority dictate that he live the life of the under-dog and play the game if he is to survive. This is particularly true whenever he encounters an officer of the law. He realizes that he has to "act out the role" and give the expected answers.

But the human being is limited in his ability to withstand the perpetual agony of physical violence, debasement, and hopelessness before something gives. For Peter this crisis comes three days after his rent had been paid by a Jewish friend named Jules. As he listens to the symphony from the radio downstairs, the crescendo of the music echoes the inward, unresolved tensions which cling to him like the plague: ". . . . the climbing soloist . . . would reach a height and everything would join him, the violins first and then the horns; and then the deep bass and the flute and the bitter trampling drums; beating, beating and mounting together and stopping with a crash like daybreak" (75). There was a knock at the door, and Peter instinctively knew—rent or no rent—that his lease had expired. He opened the door: "You get outa my house!" [the landlady screamed] "This is a white neighborhood, I don't rent to colored people. Why don't you go on uptown where you belong?" (76). And then the feeling of guilt, the vague sense of unworthiness in the face of his ejection, overwhelmed his whole being: "It was as though I had done something wrong, something monstrous, years ago, which no one had forgotten and for which I would be killed" (76 - 77).

The impact of Peter's sense of futility triggers an implosion, and the corrosive hatred born of fear arises within him: "I wanted to kill her, I watched her stupid, wrinkled white face and I wanted to take a club, a hatchet, and bring it down with all my weight, splitting her skull down the middle where she parted her iron-grey hair" (76 - 77). This implosion, this latent fury, is shared by all black people. Baldwin contends "I cannot imagine any Negro in this country who has not for at least one of the twenty-four hours of a day hated all white people just because they were on his back."[7] This hostility is vividly depicted in the subway scene. Peter observes a white boy and girl as they board the train, and he reacts internally. The girl's smile, intended for her boyfriend, fell on Peter and "died" while the vials of bitterness began to well up and overflow: "Then I hated them. I wanted to do something to make them hurt, something that would crack the pink-cheeked mask" (83). He does not know the couple personally; yet he feels a generalized, universal aversion for these people, whom he regards as symbols of white tyranny and oppression.

## A.  *Denial of Personal Worth*

Perhaps it is Peter's acute sensitivity to oppression that gives rise to the crucial situation of doubt, the threat of meaninglessness. Since the age of seven when he is first called "nigger" and is never able to understand why, Peter begins to question his worth as a person. His parents accepted the images of themselves as reflected in the white social mirror, and they learned to play the game. These hard-working people told whites what they wanted to hear, paid their rent on time, and suffered stoically the endless abuses to which they were subjected. Unable to face these daily frustrations alone, they sought refuge in the church and in the liquor store. As a boy, Peter is described by his mother as "dirty as sin," and she constantly reminds him, "You ain't never gonna be nothin' *but* a bum . . ." (72). His father before him, whom he had never seen, had also been a bum.

Thus, Peter comes from a background that reinforces the dominant myths and generalizations about black people and projects the image of blacks as being deeply religious, childishly simple-minded, excessively fond of alcohol, extremely unclean in body, and unusually lacking in ambition. Having been brainwashed, indoc-trinated, and conditioned for as long as they could remember, these black people had made the terrible and tragic mistake of believing what white people said about them.

By the time Peter is sixteen, he sees no future in his life or in the life around him, so he runs away from home. But by then, the dead-ly, numbing poison of racism has already begun to take effect: "We lived in an old shack in a town in New Jersey in the nigger part of town, the kind of houses colored people live in all over the U.S. I hated my mother for living there. I hated all the people in my neighborhood" (70).

At twenty-six Peter again comes to realize that his life has no significance, and "everyday I hated myself more. . . . I felt that I was drowning, that hatred had corrupted me like cancer in the bone" (69, 79). Consequently, his ejection brings to the surface the deep anxiety and frustration which he had harbored since childhood, and it stimulates a sense of raging futility which he dramatically tries to convey to Jules:

Goddammit to hell, I'm sick of it. Can't I get a place to sleep without dragging it through the courts? . . . I'm goddam tired of battling every Tom, Dick, and Harry for what everybody else takes for granted. I'm tired, man, tired! . . . If this goes on much longer, they'll send me to Bellevue, I'll blow my top, I'll break somebody's head. I'm not worried about that miserable little room. I'm worried about what's happening to me, *to me*, in-side. I don't walk the streets, I crawl . . . (78).

But Jules, like Peter's Irish girlfriend Ida, is representative of the white "liberal" American who is "far more hopeful, far more inno-cent, far more irresponsible, far less aware of the terrible, black, ugly facts of life than black people can afford to be. . . . "[8] Part of the rage that Peter experiences is due to the fact that he has been condemned to live amid the merciless ignorance and indifference of the vast majority of white people in this country.

## B.   *Failure of Human Relationships*

Several unsuccessful efforts are made by Jules and Ida in the course of the story to establish a channel of communication. On a driving tour, Peter and Ida pass several dilapidated shacks behind which the day's washing has been hung to dry. She questions, "Are people living there?" and Peter replies sarcastically, "Just darkies" (72). Both Ida and Jules display a shockingly superficial understanding of the black experience when they reflect on Peter's evacuation. Jules responds, "Cheer up, baby. The world's wide and life—life, she is very long" (77). Ida tries to convey a sense of fraternity between whites and blacks which Peter has long before realized does not exist: " . . . we're all in this together the whole world. Don't let it throw you. What can't be helped you have to learn to live with" (81).

Yet the "wide world," as seen from Jules' perspective, pales before Peter's view and rapidly shrinks into a dilapidated ghetto, fit not for living, but for demolition, where life, in sharp contrast to white society, is generally very *short* indeed. Ida's sense of kinship with Peter stems from the sexual gratification which she receives, and Peter becomes a big black buck rather than an individual with human needs and desires. Both Jules and Ida are as incapable of understanding Peter's predicament as he is of explaining it. He does not know why he is filled with a deadly hatred, accompanied by an overwhelming sense of guilt—guilt at his failings, guilt at his feelings, guilt at not understanding just what is happening to him or why. He does not understand the significance of his life. Yet, he does begin to realize that the enemy consists not only of the bigoted landlady and her prejudiced tenants, but also of such "well-meaning" white liberals as Jules and Ida. According to Bluefarb, they "are ineffective precisely because they try too hard to be effective. Perhaps this is true of many white liberals *vis à vis* "the problem"—they try too hard and thus turn into what I have called *white* Uncle Toms."[9]

The final, tragic realization of Peter's worthlessness comes when he aimlessly boards a subway train, "not knowing where it was going and not caring," and tries to establish a relationship with other blacks. He winds up in a Harlem bar on Seventh Avenue among blacks with whom he feels no affinity. He is certainly an outsider who lives between two worlds and is, in fact, a part of neither: "I longed for some opening, some sign, something to make me a part of the life around me. But there was nothing except my color. . . . I didn't seem to have a place" (84).

After his brutal experiences in the white world, Peter is unable to find a place for himself, even in Harlem, where he is regarded with incomprehension and suspicion. As Bluefarb perceptively points out, Peter's crisis symbolizes the very crux of the "double-jeopardy" dilemma facing black intellectuals in America today: ". . . he is too bright and sensitive for the black Harlem milieu of bars and honky-tonks and too black for the white world whether 'liberal' or racist. Peter stands between the two, though unable to bridge the gap between them."[10]

### IV   Breaking the Chain: Strategy, Survival, and Freedom

Baldwin continues his probe of the estrangement of the black intellectual in "This Morning, This Evening, So Soon." In this story we encounter the artist as singer who functions as first-person narrator in revealing his story of success in Europe. This triumph, however, is contrasted sharply with constant "nightmares" and inner feelings of frustration and alienation, the majority of which can be traced back to the singer's youth.

As we learn through a series of flashbacks, the narrator, like Peter, had been reared by parents whose traditional values served as reinforcements of the *status quo*. This was the facade which had been erected painfully with but one objective in view: survival. Consequently, the artist had inherited a life fraught with anxiety; he had acquired the ability to attune himself emotionally to the demands of white society: "I had once known how to pitch my voice precisely between curtness and servility, and known what razor's edge of a pickaninny's smile would turn away wrath" (141).

His experiences with the police corroborate the encounters with the law which Peter reveals in "Previous Condition," and they serve as a symbol of the thousands of indignities and humiliations which the masses of blacks face on a day-to-day basis. The narrator recalls that in his hometown in Alabama, typically, a police car might pull up to the curb. And, being black, you realize that you have been called to appear before the law—judge, jury, and executioner—to answer the charge of drunkenness. Any defense offered that fails to elicit laughter and manifestations of amusement—any slight deviation from the expected mode of conduct—will literally heap wrath and fury upon your head: "The trick is to think of some way for them to have their fun without beating you up. . . . And they'll do anything at all, to prove that you're no better than a dog and to make you feel like one" (150).

Having "survived" these experiences, the narrator travels to Europe to pursue his career and to escape "the menacing, the hostile, killing world" into which he was born. At this point the autobiographical element becomes evident. Baldwin tells us that "I left America because I doubted my ability to survive the fury of the color problem here,"[11] and so he, like the protagonist, escapes to Europe in an effort to recover a sense of his uniqueness, to begin his quest for identity. The author's description of his exhilaration, his sense of freedom, his feeling, "for the first time in his life—that he can reach out to everyone, that he is accessible to everyone and open to everything,"[12] parallels the narrator's jubilation on the April morning, high upon the Pont Royal Bridge, when he discovers his love for Harriet. But as he describes that moment, he reveals a parallel and equally engulfing electrification as the awareness dawns upon him that he is free; the white man is no longer on his back: "There were millions of people all around us, but I was alone with Harriet. She was alone with me. Never, in all my life, until that moment, had I been alone with anyone. . . . During all the years of my life, until that moment, I had carried the menacing, hostile, killing world with me everywhere" (135).

Thus, there is a feeling of release and relief; the tension is gone, and he has found love, peace, and tranquility in Paris, "the city which saved my life . . . by allowing me to find out who I am" (135). The whiteness of Harriet's skin and the darkness of his own were of no consequence. Here, at last, was a society that made no effort to circumscribe his feelings, his behavior, his very existence. He was free to discover the meaning of his life and become a man.

Then came the death of his mother, followed by a three-month return visit to America. During those four years in Europe, he had violated the two basic canons in the code of conduct that he had learned so well as a child. First, he had gone North and to Europe, experienced a different society, and forgotten how to shuffle his feet, scratch his head, and cater to the whims of the white power structure. Secondly, refusing to restrict his amorous inclinations to his own race, he had fallen in love with Harriet. For the first offense, he could be whipped in line, beaten, and "put in his place"; but for the second transgression, the violation of lily-white womanhood, there would have been—had they known—only one possible punishment: castration and death. Intuitively he knew these things.

With the approach of New York, "slowly and patiently, like some enormous, cunning, and murderous beast, ready to devour, impossible to escape . . ." (140) came the realization that the white passengers were moving with the boat toward freedom and safety;

only he was approaching the danger and insecurity of his native land. And if one iota of doubt about the cruciality of that impending danger remained, the fat, red-faced cop standing below the plank shouted a grim reaffirmation of that fact: "Come on, boy, . . . come on, come on!" (142).

That summer he had been "lucky" enough to get a job running an elevator in a large department store through the "kindness" of white friends, but it had not worked out because he no longer believed what white people said about him: "People kept saying, I hope you didn't bring no foreign notions back here with you, boy. And I'd say, 'No sir,' or 'No M'am,' but I never said it right. And there was a time, all of them remembered it, when I *had* said it right. But now they could tell that I despised them—I guess, no matter what, I wanted them to know that I despised them. But I didn't despise them any more than everyone else did, only the others never let it show" (150). There was simply no way to reconcile his childhood patterns of traditional behavior with the freedom that he had experienced in Paris. He could no longer attune his hopes, fears, desires, and aspirations to the prejudices of white society. He had forgotten the rules of life and death in the game of survival which the black man in America is compelled to play: "That moment on the bridge had undone me forever" (141).

That had been eight years ago, and yet the horrible nightmare lingers hauntingly as the singer again prepares to make the trip across the Atlantic—this time with his wife and his young son, Paul. He has become famous now, and that fame—like all achievement—requires nourishment by an unbroken line of future successes. The prospect of singing on the nightclub circuit and the beckon of Hollywood lights combined to lure him from his new, secure life in Paris. And yet, neither fame, nor bright lights, nor fortune can dispel the ugly reality of the nightmare, the hatred, the fear.

Harriet jokes with Paul that his father has become worried about the reception which he will receive in New York. She reassures her husband, innocently, that things are never as bad as they seem. But she does not know the unspeakable horror, the degradation, and the humiliation that attend the very survival of the black man in America. And he has good reason to fear—not that they will not like his songs—not even that they will require him to give up his life. What he fears most is that these indignities suffered by him and by his father and his father's father since time immemorial will be heaped upon the innocent head of his son, working their way into his psyche and corrupting his very being: ". . . I discovered that I did not want my son ever to feel toward me as I had felt toward my own father. . . . I had watched the humiliations he had to bear, and I had pitied him. . . .

But for Paul, I swore it, such a day would never come. I would throw my life and my work between Paul and the nightmare of the world. I would make it impossible for the world to treat Paul as it had treated my father and me" (148 - 149). Indeed, this is an ambitious undertaking when one is journeying to a "new world," especially when that new world is America and the color of one's skin is black.

## V   Burden of Blackness

We have seen Baldwin at his best in presenting several different facets of alienation in *Going to Meet the Man:* alienation from one's culture ("Sonny's Blues"), alienation from one's people ("Previous Condition"), and alienation from one's country ("This Morning, This Evening, So Soon"). Still a fourth aspect of estrangement dominates the action in "Come Out of the Wilderness": alienation from self.

When we meet Ruth Bowman, nine years have passed since her "nightmare," but she remembers the traumatic confrontation as if it were yesterday. Her brother had slipped into the barn and discovered Ruth and her lover in a moment of youthful, innocent caresses. He had mistakenly imagined them guilty of fornication, and her father had made the same assumption. The boy had been beaten severely. She, too, had felt several physical blows in the confusion, but it was the psychological injury from which she never completely recovered. Ruth had proclaimed their innocence, and yet no one understood. Until this day, Ruth had been haunted by the judgment that her family had made: "You dirty . . . you dirty . . . you black and dirty— . . . and she felt dirty, she felt that nothing would ever make her clean" (181). This situation is described from a psychoanalytical point of view by Joseph Vollmerhausen as a neurotic process which results in the truncation and perversion of the total personality: "The neurotic process begins in a climate adverse to the growth of the child as an individual. Such unfavorable conditions are rarely, if ever singular traumatic experiences, but are found in the family atmosphere.

They manifest themselves in a gross and subtle disregard for the needs and possibilities of the child. The parents have their own overriding compulsive needs and egocentricities which hinder them from perceiving and conceptualizing their child as the particular individual he is."[13] In this environment, it is not unusual for the child to suffer from a lack of security normally provided by belongingness and togetherness, and to develop feelings of hostility and estrangement.

In spite of her father's insistence, Ruth maintained her innocence and refused to "cry repentance." She could not accept the guilt which everyone thought should be laid at her door. Her immediate efforts were directed toward emotional withdrawal, but finally, after repeated recriminations, she began to feel a strange compulsion to accept that vague sense of guilt and to seek the means of atonement through suffering.

The first liaison, she recalls, was with Arthur, a black musician who took her away to New York. Their relationship lasted four years, but it was unsatisfactory in many ways—mainly because Arthur failed to corroborate the image of worthlessness which she had accepted for herself. Arthur had sent her to school to study business, and it was chiefly through his efforts that Ruth had begun to overcome the feeling that she was "black and unattractive." He had tried to help Ruth to build a positive self-image, to destroy the negative perception, but he had only succeeded in creating anxiety, the confusion of an ambivalent self-concept in her mind. At the time of the dissolution of their relationship, however, the positive image dominated, and it was not until Ruth's encounter with Paul that this ambivalence became apparent.

The second brief love affair with the merchant seaman was also a disaster. Perhaps this lover might have fulfilled the need to suffer, and he might have become her "Paul." But there was no need for suffering now. Ruth's positive image continued to prevail, and she would not be hurt and abused by her young lover, according to his fancy. She would not be abused as if she were Mister Charlie's slave and he the master's son. And yet, things might have been different if Paul had never walked into her life.

She had met her "Michelangelo" in Greenwich Village, and there had been happiness at first. And then, amid Paul's irregular comings and goings, loneliness began to overwhelm her. She could remember many nights when "she lay there on a bed that inexorably became a bed of ashes and hot coals, while her imagination dwelt on every conceivable disaster, from his having forsaken her for another woman to his having, somehow, ended up in the morgue. . . . There were places she could have called, but she would have died first. After all—he had only needed to point it out once, he would never have occasion to point it out again—they were not married" (171).

Ruth had become involved with Paul, and somehow the dark, cold reality had condemned her dreams to semi-obliteration. She had envisioned herself as a wife and mother, married to a "great, slow, black man" who was able to provide a measure of stability for her life. Ruth would make a home for him, bear his children, and enjoy the peace and comfort which would be her fortress against the harsh realities of life. Still clinging to the faded remnants of that dream, she regretted the day when Paul walked into her life. He had become the trap from which she was unable to escape. Grier and Cobbs explain this masochistic tendency in their discussion of a similar case history: ". . . It is clear that it was necessary for her to suffer in a particular way to experience sexual pleasure. . . . In her associations she saw herself as a black, ugly, ignorant, dirty little girl who could be loved by no one. She fairly wallowed in the perception of herself as such a creature with degraded sexual appetites. She fancied herself . . . as a helpless sex object available to contemptuous white men at their whim."[14]

At twenty-six, it would seem that Ruth could, by an act of simple volition, walk out of "the wilderness" into the promise of a new life of happiness, security, and stability. But she remained powerless to act. This ambiguity—the inability to choose between a traumatic reality and the need to search for self-realization and fulfillment—is clearly manifested throughout the story. As she and Paul lay in bed, Baldwin compares her desire for him to that of ". . . a river trying to run two ways at once: she felt herself shirking from him, yet she flowed toward him too . . ." (175). It is precisely this dichotomy which Fromm-Reichmann describes as an insurmountable block to the achievement of identity: "This inability to learn to replace old patterns by new ones deprives a person of the freedom to live and move about in the world of psychological reality, deprives him of the freedom for self-realization and conveys feelings of stagnation and sterility. . . ."[15]

Since she began living with Paul, Ruth's life had become riddled with loneliness, frustration, and hatred. Frequently she awoke in the morning, "cold" and "trembling," only to find herself alone.

Hurrying to the office, Ruth became confident that he would call later in the day, and she would be prepared: "She would have had several stiff drinks and so could be very offhand over the phone, pretending that she had only supposed him to have gotten up a little earlier than herself that morning. But the moment she put the receiver down she hated him. . . . She had tried hard to want other men . . . but all she knew about other men was that they were not Paul" (171 - 172). Her boss, Mr. Davis, might have become her black liberator, but by the time his interest became apparent, Ruth's sense of guilt and shame had already overwhelmed her. Besides, he could not inflict the pain, the misery, the suffering which would help her atone for her guilt. Only the cruel white master could do that. Though she yearned for a love that would free her from that childhood burden, she knew that Paul's touch would never serve that end: "He had power over her not because she was free but because she was guilty. To enforce his power over her he had only to keep her guilt awake . . . for his own convenience" (187). His love had lifted her to the heights of happiness, only to send her plummeting to the depths of despair; she became more unclean than ever as she lay in his arms: "And yet—she went into his arms with such eagerness and such hope. . . . She was punishing herself for something, a crime she could not remember. *You dirty . . . you black and dirty . . .* (187)."

Ruth could never be free. She had been judged guilty, and her sentence had been fixed. And until that glorious day of liberation—if, indeed, such a day would ever come—she must hurry through the crowds "to hide from them and from herself the fact that she did not know where she was going" (197).

## VI    *The White Problem: Power*

The question of guilt becomes a dominant thematic concern in the title story of the collection, "Going to Meet the Man," as Baldwin probes into the black experience through the warped, perverted mind of a white deputy sheriff in a small Southern town. This perspective is useful here because it provides us with an insight into the distorted reality upon which the white psyche depends. It further supports Baldwin's assumption that, ". . . before one can really talk about the Negro problem in this country, one has to talk about the white people's problem."[16] One has to know the history behind the invention of the American "nigger" and he must realize that this device, indeed, like all other inventions, grew out of necessity and expedience. Consequently, the "nigger" became the ego-crutch, the nourishment by which white security and superiority were fed at the table of black instability and inferiority. He became a negative criterion which furnished the white social structure with coherence: "You can almost say—you can say, in fact—that one of the reasons that the Negro is at the bottom of the social heap in America, is because it's the only way everyone in America will know where the bottom is."[17] The question is WHY? Why has it been necessary for one people to destroy—physically and emotionally—another people and to make every ruthless effort to obscure and obliterate that people's contribution to western civilization? It is this question—yet unanswered—on which Baldwin sheds a ray of light in "Going to Meet the Man" as he analyzes the crucial anxieties and frustrations of the white mind in the South. In examining these inner conflicts, Baldwin considers two aspects of this problem: the challenge of power and the challenge of sex.

In this story the festive atmosphere of a picnic contrasts sharply with the merciless lynching-castration of a black man and provides a focal point for Baldwin's analysis of the impact that this experience has had on the consciousness of a young white boy, now grown to be a man. Jesse began working in the small town as a mail-order salesman, and he had done his job well: selling inferior merchandise to unsuspecting blacks. And when he had become adept at the *physical* robbery of black people, when he had demonstrated his acceptance of the white-perpetuated myths and illusions about blacks, he was promoted by society to engage in the *psychological* theft of black pride and dignity. Jesse became a deputy sheriff, and he had gotten used to the job.

One night as he lay in bed, unable to make sexual contact with his wife, he began to recall his activities of the previous day. The leader of a black voter registration drive and his followers had been jailed for disturbing the peace, and Jesse had been dispatched to put an end to the singing among the prisoners by torturing the leader: "I put the prod to him and he jerked some more and he kind of screamed—but he didn't have much voice left. . . . The boy rolled around in his own dirt and water and blood and tried to scream again as the prod hit his testicles, but the scream did not come out, only a kind of rattle and moan" (201 - 202). He could not understand the niggers. They had been obedient enough in the past, until the Northerners put some crazy ideas into their heads.

He didn't want to beat the niggers; he was a peace-loving man, but "he was only doing his duty . . . [and he knew] that what he was doing was right—he knew that, nobody had to tell him that . . ." (204 - 205).

Throughout his life he had tried to live according to the laws of God and man. Since birth he had been honor-bound to defend the *status quo*, and he could not sit idly by while the niggers destroyed the myths and illusions which made up his distorted view of reality and the reality of white society as well. And yet, what he does not realize is that what is at issue is not the destruction of social values but the psychological self-annihilation of the man himself. As he recalls the cattle-prodding incident, he remembers that "he was shaking worse than the boy had been shaking. . . . the singing filled him as though it were a weird, uncontrollable, monstrous howling rumbling up from the depths of his own belly, he felt an icy fear rise in him and raise him up . . ." (202, 204).

This is the anxiety which drives Jesse. It is a morbid, uncontrollable fear of all individuals who dare to challenge the white power structure. It is the trepidation that black people will somehow rise *en masse* to take control of their own affairs. This apprehensiveness, which is basic to segregation and to the American way of life, is based on the triumph of right, as defined exclusively within the white context. Those who have different physical appearances, or who are motivated by different ideological persuasions become threats to the Established Order, and therefore they must be destroyed. It becomes extremely difficult, therefore, for whites to tolerate any culture, except to the extent that it mirrors their own.

## VII    *The White Problem: Sex*

The challenge of power is no more serious a threat than the challenge of sex. Here, as in *Blues for Mister Charlie* and elsewhere, Baldwin suggests that white men find the black female sexually attractive because of the appeal of the forbidden and the illicit. It is she who is forced to cater to those sexual fantasies which lie beyond the dignity of his white sex partner. This attitude becomes evident very early in the story when Jesse finds himself unable to make love to his wife:

He could not ask her to do just a little thing for him, just to help him out, just for a little while, the way he could ask a nigger girl to do

it. . . . Sometimes, sure, like any other man, he knew that he wanted a little more spice than Grace could give him and he would drive over yonder
and pick up a black piece or arrest her, it came to the same
thing. . . . What had the good Lord Almighty had in mind when he made
the niggers? Well. They were pretty good at that, all right. Damn. Damn,.
Goddam (198 - 199).

Jesse's attitude toward the virtue of black women is typical of the
white man's attitude in general. The black girl or woman becomes
merely a sexual tool, a means of expediency through which he can
conduct his sexual experimentations and release his tensions and
frustrations while the black male—husband or lover—stands im-
potently on the sidelines, gripped by the twin self-destructive
monsters of fear and hate. And yet, if white men are free to exploit
black women sexually, is it not possible that white women, equally
lured by contact with the forbidden, might become attracted to
black men? Might it not be that black men, similarly motivated,
secretly desire white flesh and stand in waiting for every opportunity to violate the pure white flower of womanhood? "Thus began the
myth of the male Negro's sexuality and the great fear of it. And thus
began the vicious circle—white people seeing what they feared was
there. This, of course, so often provides the necessary challenge to
Negroes to live up to the myth: in short, what Robert Merton would
describe as a self-fulfilling prophecy in which 'confident error
generates its own spurious confirmation.'"[18]
This sheds some light on the white man's obsessive preoccupation
with the black male genitalia, symbolic embodiment of the myth of
black sexual superiority, and on his determination to destroy the sex
organ as the singular means of inhibiting the violation of white
womanhood. This explains, further, the sheer delight which Jesse's
father and his friends found in watching the castration which Jesse
so vividly describes: "The man with the knife took the nigger's
privates in his hand, one hand, still smiling, as though he were
weighing them. . . . The white hand stretched them, cradled
them, caressed them. Then the dying man's eyes looked straight
into Jesse's eyes—it could not have been as long as a second, but it
seemed longer than a year. Then Jesse screamed as the knife flash-
ed, first up, then down, cutting the dreadful thing away, and the
blood came roaring down" (216).
We, like Jesse, are not certain for what reason this man had been
condemned to die. But, given the myth of black male sexual

superiority, it might have been any "crime" from looking at a white woman (generally considered to be a manifestation of sexual desire) to the most despicable of crimes—the sex act itself—which is invariably interpreted as "rape," regardless of the circumstances surrounding the situation. It is not by accident, then, that the penalty for rape in this country is death, although the record shows that precious few white men have ever been convicted of the rape of black women.

But the crimes wrought upon the oppressed wreak havoc upon the victimizers as well. Sex, then, for Baldwin, comes to symbolize fruition, a consummating process in the lives of human beings. The black man has had his genitalia removed, and thus he has been cut off from this achievement. Yet, Jesse, too, has been emasculated, from an emotional perspective. He has been consumed by hate, and consequently, his sexual impotence symbolizes the incompleteness resulting from this corruption. Jesse is fustrated because he cannot determine the meaning of his suffering. Psychologically, he, too—even though temporarily—has had his sex removed. His inadequacy in consummating the sex act symbolizes his inability to look at himself and recognize the ugly, unspeakable crimes which he has perpetrated in the name of white supremacy.

If there is a theme that runs through *Going to Meet the Man*, perhaps it is the "white problem," not the black situation. The great crime, then, is that whites have become so firmly established in their perverted values and distorted sense of reality that they have become blind to the terror of their deeds. The calamity is a white tragedy, and what is at issue is not whether the dichotomous system created by the duality of first and second-class citizenship will continue to prevail. What is at stake is whether or not this country can ever uproot the fantasies embedded in its most cherished traditions and institutions and recover its sense of reality which has been buried beneath the sands of racism for so long.

The characters in these stories have been drawn from the masses of society, through whom Baldwin is able to evaluate the entire range of his own unique experiences. Consequently, the stories presented here become artistic endeavors to discover that territory where human communication and intercourse can dwell, unhampered by the hostilities of prejudice and racism. And Baldwin's urgent message is conveyed in clear, precise, and unequivocal terms: It is this upon which our survival depends.

CHAPTER 3

# Love Denied, Love Fulfilled

### I  Reaching for Self: Chaos and Futility

WHEN we consider that Baldwin's European self-exile was motivated chiefly by a quest for self-perception, it is not at all
surprising that he employs the confessional mode in his first novel,
*Go Tell It on the Mountain*.[1] Using the fictional character John
Grimes as a surrogate, Baldwin begins his unrestrained, perceptive
probe into his own frustrations and the shortcoming of his family as
a whole. Like Robert Lowell and Norman Mailer, Baldwin clearly
assumes that confusion, blindness, and corruption are universal evils
and that a candid acknowledgment of his own deficiencies promotes
a universal understanding of those inadequacies in others: "The
questions which one asks oneself begin, at last, to illuminate the
world, and become one's key to the experience of others. One can
only face in others what one can face in oneself. On this confrontation depends the measure of our wisdom and compassion. This
energy is all that one finds in the rubble of vanished civilizations,
and the only hope for ours."[2]

For Baldwin, one's "energy" to conduct a candid, introspective
examination leads ultimately to a linking of the personal and the
universal experiences. It is this same baring of one's soul that Walt
Whitman accomplished in *Leaves of Grass*. Ignoring the puritan
sensibilities of his audience, Whitman ventured to abandon conven-
tion and give full expression to his inner feelings:

> I will therefore let flame from me the burning fires
>    that were threatening to consume me,
> I will lift what has too long kept down those smoldering fires,
> I will give them complete abandonment. . . .[3]

Like Whitman's poem, Baldwin's novel becomes an exorcism, a

50

purgation, a necessary constriction which leads, ultimately, to the unlimited expanses of self-identity.

*Go Tell* stands as an honest, intensive, self-analysis, functioning simultaneously to illuminate self, society, and mankind as a whole. It is a quest that ends in futility for all of the characters except John Grimes because they are unable to achieve two Baldwinian prerequisites for self-discovery: the understanding necessary for an acceptance of the past and the ability to establish genuine interpersonal relationships among humanity. Let us examine these characters from this perspective.

It is interesting to note that Baldwin has chosen to present these self-truths in a religious context. As we look further, a pattern seems to emerge, for we find theological overtones in other works, notably "The Rockpile," "The Outing," *The Amen Corner, Blues for Mister Charlie,* and *If Beale Street Could Talk,* as well as in numerous essays. Yet, curiously enough, he contends that ". . . the standards which come from Greece and Rome, from the Judeo-Christian ethic, are very dubious when you try to apply them to your own life."[4] This apparent paradox, however, is grounded in the differentiation which Baldwin makes between the "Judeo-Christian ethic" and the emotional fervor generated by the spirituals and the blues (he makes no distinction) which grew out of our acceptance of that ethic and formed the basis of the history of the black man in America. We must never reject the messages of Bessie Smith, Aretha Franklin, or Ray Charles because they sing of the past, for the past provides an indispensable link of coherence with the present. Robert K. Bingham also succinctly corroborates Baldwin's point of view in his argument that ethnic individuality should not be denied: "The Negro, who of all immigrants arrived with the least baggage, has built out of what he found here—even out of slavery—something that has beauty and dignity. Too many whites ignore it out of mistaken politeness, and too many Negroes ignore it out of mistaken shame."[5]

A. *Struggle with the Past*

Of all the characters in *Go Tell*, it is Florence who is guilty of "mistaken shame." As she sits among the congregation of the Temple of the Fire Baptized, Florence becomes silently critical of the spiritual fervor which she observes among the members. Even as a girl, she hated the "indecent practice" of the "common niggers" who screamed and wept and prostrated themselves before the altar; she could never stoop so low. Florence had never prayed. As a child, she had been forced to kneel while her mother prayed, but her thoughts were always directed toward her brother Gabriel's destruction. And even tonight, as she kneels at the altar to pray for the divine healing of her disease-ridden body, her preoccupations are mundane. For years she had held Deborah's letter which recounted Gabriel's brief affair with Esther, hoping to use it as an instrument for accomplishing Gabriel's humiliation and perdition which, in her opinion, were long overdue. In her heart she regrets that her chance will never come. It is ironic that in the midst of her own pain and suffering, her sole reflections are those of inflicting anguish and distress upon others.

Florence is incapable of sustaining a genuine human relationship because she is unable to love. From the day he was born, she had begun to despise Gabriel because he had stolen her birthright. Her hope for an education and a few of the comforts of life had been "swallowed up" as Mrs. Grimes began to shower her attention and her meager resources on her son. Florence had also been deeply affected by her friend Deborah's multiple rape by a band of white men, and she had decided that all men are driven by a brutal, humiliating lust which seeks to dissipate itself in sexual gratification. And as Gabriel grew into manhood, he had come to symbolize that degrading, animal-like passion of the flesh. Vividly she remembered the bacchanal-natured, youthful Gabriel, staggering home after an evening of debauchery, and the corrosive, hostile fires began to kindle and then rage within until she could no longer restrain herself: "I hate him! I hate him! Big, black prancing tomcat of a nigger!" (75). Bound fast in the desolate valley of hate, she had never gained the strength to climb the mountain and know the joys of love.

Frank had seemed different and Florence had married him with the hope of the material comforts which she so desperately desired. He would buy a home and take her away from the inferior blacks who lived nearby. This materialistic obsession had been the object of her life, although Frank did not share that goal. In spite of her, he cherished a kinship with their neighbors, and he had been content to live among them, realizing that they were "coming along" and that, for many of them, this process would never be completed. Florence had learned this lesson, but she had never been able to identify her husband as one of those people. By temperament, she was totally unfit to bring to the marriage the love, compassion, and understanding that Frank needed. And so, after ten years of marriage, he had walked out of the door, never to return.

That had been twenty years ago. Having deserted her mother in her hour of need, having mocked Gabriel's ministry and Deborah's barrenness, having denied Frank the need for conjugal communication, she comes to the end of her life, forlorn and unfulfilled. As her body has been racked with disease, so her heart has been corrupted by the hatred which she has nourished in her breast.

## B.  *Struggle with the Flesh*

If Florence's life is filled with hostility, perhaps Gabriel's existence can only be described as lustful and selfish. He had become involved with three "fallen" women, always for the purpose of satisfying his own egotistical desires. Gabriel married Deborah because he fancied himself her divinely appointed savior, sent "to raise her up, to release her from that dishonor which was hers in the eyes of men" (109). In turn, she, the virgin, would give him the son to continue his "royal" line. But there had been barrenness, and no heir had come forth.

This unproductiveness of the marital bed is symbolic of the sterility of the conjugal relationship that existed between Gabriel and Deborah. Given his air of condescension, it is anything but surprising that their relationship never reached the ground of mutuality. He was the holy man, the deliverer, and she, the handmaiden, had been chosen for her meekness and humility to do his bidding. Subsequently, we have what Baldwin has referred to as a "breakdown of communication between the sexes."[6] Deborah becomes a millstone hung about Gabriel's neck, a burden to be borne in the heat of the day. Thus, the failure of their relationship results from this "breakdown" which rejects the possibility of identity achievement for both partners.

Perhaps, from a psychological viewpoint, it is this dissatisfaction that leads Gabriel to Esther. Gabriel had invited her to church, and he had prayed that she would forsake her licentious and dissolute ways and come to God. Once again, he assumes the role of deliverer. He wants to save her from "the destruction so ardently pursued—to fold her in him and hide her until the wrath of God was past," (125) but he was weak. Gabriel felt the "lions of lust" rush through his body again for the first time since his conversion, and he was undone. The affair had lasted only nine nights, but the royal heir had already begun to grow in Esther's womb. Incapable of compassion, he had sent her off to Chicago and allowed her to die in childbirth. And then, having gone North after Deborah's death, he met Elizabeth.

Gabriel could not own Esther's son Royal, and therefore his house was yet without an heir. Florence had introduced him to Elizabeth, and he had shown an interest in her young, nameless son, a living testimony to her shame and sin. It was Gabriel who had been sent to redeem her: " . . . I done come, and it was the hand of the Lord what sent me" (187). These words, strikingly allusive to Christ's declaration in John 10:10 that "I have come that they might have life and that they might have it more abundantly," clearly indicate the role of deliverer that Gabriel attempts to assume. He has been "sent" as a redeemer, but, unlike Christ, he is by temperament ill-fitted for the task.

Just as Esther had satisfied his desires of the flesh, so Elizabeth had been called upon to fulfill the role for which Deborah had found herself inadequate. Like the two women before her, Elizabeth became merely the means by which the necessary end was accomplished. And it was only through the painful lessons of the years that she began to realize that she was not Gabriel's wife; she was only the mother of his son, Roy.

And yet it is Gabriel himself who is desperately in need of redemption; he stands in need of deliverance from himself. He preaches his sermons, makes love to his prostitutes, and marries his women—all for the convenience of the moment. He is as incapable of pursuing his own quest for identity as he is of assisting these women in discovering theirs because he has lost touch with humanity. The most glaring evidence of this shortcoming is nowhere more obvious than in his failure to establish a genuine relationship with his two sons. After Esther's death, Royal returns to live with his grandmother in the south. Gabriel had secretly prayed that Royal might be saved from the reckless life he was beginning to lead, but he could not bring himself to reach out to his young son who was struggling frantically—even as Gabriel himself had struggled—against the temptations of the flesh. And had he known, subconsciously, the reason for his rejection of Royal, Gabriel could never have admitted it, even to himself: Royal's life had been a re-creation of the profligate life which he himself had led in his youth. He had striven desperately, since his conversion, to force from his consciousness those wanton adventures of earlier years. There had been but one fall from grace, and Royal became a living witness to his sin. But Gabriel had become a holy man whose life had been dedicated to the service of God, and he could never permit these facts to cross the threshold of reality. Instead, he stood by, allowing Royal's debauchery to destroy him in expiation of the guilt which Gabriel felt about the circumstances surrounding the boy's conception.

When Elizabeth gave birth to Roy, Gabriel prayed that he might one day follow in his father's footsteps in the church, but Roy had inherited his father's youthful waywardness, and he had no designs on the ministry whatsoever. Early in Part One of the novel, we find Roy stretched out on the sofa after having received a superficial knife wound in a fight. Gabriel, incoherent with anger and grief, alternately blames John and "white folks," placing the ultimate responsibility for the deed on Elizabeth. Never does he even suggest that Roy is at fault because he cannot acknowledge the deeds of his own past, reenacted by Royal and resurrected again in Roy.

Gabriel Grimes had never been able to communicate with his young son because he perceived Roy merely as the means to the end of continuing the royal line. Unable to understand the boy's lack of enthusiasm for the vocation chosen for him, Gabriel seeks to force his will on the unyielding youth. He cannot look upon Roy as a wayward boy in need of finding the means of establishing a father-son relationship. It is this insensitivity that leads Roy to turn to Elizabeth for the understanding which Gabriel has failed to provide: " . . .tell me how come he don't never let me talk to him like I talk to you? He's my father, ain't he? But he don't never listen to me—no, I all the time got to listen to him" (25). But there can be no recognition of Roy's need; there can be no communication. Gabriel is incapable of these things because love has never become a reality in his life.

## C. *Coming to Grips with the Void*

Just as Florence and Gabriel had learned to hate, so Elizabeth also hated as a child. She hated her mother for what she assumed to be her inability to love her darker child. Later Elizabeth had learned to respond to her aunt with a "cancerous" hatred and fear. But, more importantly, she had known the redemption of love. Her father had been kind and generous, and he had returned his daughter's love. The toys, the pretty clothes, the Sunday strolls, the trips to the circus, and the Punch and Judy shows—all of these, in her young mind, attested to her father's love. Yet it had been her fate, after the death of her mother, to suffer the untimely and disastrous separation from her father, from the only love that she had ever known.

In spite of Elizabeth's removal from the object of her affection, she retained the *capacity* to love. Then one day Richard walked into her life and filled the terrible void left by her father. She and her lover had left Maryland for New York, and they planned to be married when enough money had been saved. Richard had given her love and captured her heart: "She lived, in those days, in a fiery storm, of which Richard was the center and the heart. And she fought only to reach him—only that; she was afraid only of what might happen if they were kept from one another . . ." (161). But in all too short a time, once again, the nightmare of premature separation had come upon her. Having been arrested and brutally beaten for a crime of which he was completely innocent, Richard slashed his wrists and died "among the scarlet sheets." Now Elizabeth was forced to cope with the dual realization that her lover was dead and that she must somehow summon the courage to give birth to Richard's child.

The Reverend Gabriel Grimes, she had come to believe, had been sent to deliver her and young John from their awesome loneliness and bring joy into their lives. Gabriel had kept his promise to provide the boy with his physical and spiritual needs, but he was never able to offer the sensitive child the love that was so vital to his being. Roy had always been his father's favorite, and John had learned to hate him. John knew that Gabriel secretly resented his inclination toward the ministry, and he had never been able to forget Gabriel's bitterness, particularly manifested in the minister's reaction to Roy's wound. John had seen in his stepfather's countenance a cruel, vindictive hatred, directed toward him because it was Roy, not John, who lay writhing in pain from the gash that permanently separated one of his eyebrows. As he contemplated the disaster, John was scarcely able to resist the sudden urge to smile in expression of his supreme pleasure that Roy might die and thereby "bring his father low." John's hatred for Gabriel had become so intense that he entertained with great relish the thought that he would, one day, seize the opportunity to curse Gabriel on his deathbed.

Like his mother, John had probed the bottomless pits of hatred, but he had also known the love which Baldwin depicts as a physical attraction between Elisha and John. This relationship contrasts sharply with the presentation of heterosexuality in the novel, and characteristically, as Macebuh points out, Baldwin tips the scales in favor of homosexuality: " . . . heterosexual copulation in this novel, as in Baldwin's other novels, is described often as a brutal, indecent spectacle. When Deborah is raped, or when Gabriel makes love to her later, when he sleeps with Esther or the woman from the North, and when John observes his parents in bed, it is always as though we are watching an ugly, distasteful show. The beauty of John's love for Elisha lies, then, apparently in the absence of copulation. . . ."[7] This distinction, according to Macebuh, reflects a "personal preference" of Baldwin. Yet it is also significant that he turns to Elisha after he finds himself totally unable to establish a single genuine relationship between himself and the other characters in the novel. Only Elisha is able to function as a father-surrogate for John because Elisha, unlike Gabriel, is attuned to the young boy's needs as John searches for his own identity.

## D. *Escape, Fear, and Divine Wrath*

One of the dominant motifs recurring throughout *Go Tell It on the Mountain* is that of escape. Early in the novel John whispers to Ruth that she should grow up and "run away from *this* house, run far away, . . ." (43) and after Gabriel strikes Elizabeth during the confusion surrounding Roy's accident, John feels the need to take flight " . . . as though he had encountered in the jungle some evil beast, crouching and ravenous, with eyes like Hell unclosed . . ." (48). Florence's youthful desire is to escape the sordid, desolate life led by black people, "to walk out one morning through the cabin door, never to return" (72). Gabriel sought to avoid the "betraying lust that lived in him," (95) and Elizabeth possessed a determination that hung "like a heavy jewel between her breasts . . . written in fire on the dark sky of her mind . . ." (157) to escape the aura of lovelessness which surrounded her aunt's house.

Closely related to the motif of escape is the theme of fear. All of Baldwin's characters hate; few of them are able to love. And it is precisely this failure to love which influences their concept of God as the wrathful, vindictive Being of Jonathan Edwards' Calvinistic imagination. They project their own evil natures on the Divinity, recreate God in their own images, and reduce Him to human terms. He becomes the vengeful Judge of the Old Testament rather than the loving Father of the New. Hence, each character is obsessed with fear, and each finds refuge in religion as a means of escaping that fear. John Grimes fears that the consequences of his sin of masturbation have consigned him to burn in hell forever. Florence is motivated in part by the fear of her impending death, and Gabriel fears the evil of his lustful body. Elizabeth has never repented her life with Richard, and she fears that this transgression stands between her and salvation.

For all of these people, the wrath of God becomes a double-edged sword, not only capable of accomplishing their destruction, but equally able to heap misfortune upon the heads of their enemies. It is John who hopes that Roy will die to bring his father low, and Florence clings to Deborah's letter, hoping that God will give her the opportunity to accomplish that same end. Esther is confident that Gabriel will be punished, though she is unaware of the time or the means by which her prophecy will come to pass. Elizabeth's aunt invokes a similar imprecation upon her head because the young girl refuses to submit to her will. Thus, becoming one of God's anointed serves the dual and simultaneous purpose of protection of one's own life and the destruction of one's adversaries. It is this concept of God that lies at the root of these people's inability to establish meaningful personal relationships and to find sustenance for their lives through the exhilarating power of love.

## II    The Creative Realm: A Dilemma of Sexuality

Baldwin's "personal preference" for homosexuality as a vehicle for the expression of love becomes even more pronounced in his second novel, Giovanni's Room.[8] And it is this tendency that Eldridge Cleaver seizes upon as a basis for his criticism of Baldwin in Soul on Ice. In this discussion, however, Cleaver fails to differentiate between his appraisal of Baldwin's artistic creation and of Baldwin the man. Consequently, the autobiographical element becomes as valuable a criterion as the work of art itself. It follows, then, that Cleaver's condemnation of Baldwin's artistry is based, in part, on the homosexual theme which recurs in many of his writings. The argument which Cleaver pursues here, in its broadest sense, involves one of the fundamental and enduring concerns of the literary craftsman: the question of artistic dominion. In his famous essay, "The Art of Fiction" (1888), Henry James explores this issue and makes a cogent argument for the freedom of the novelist to use his experience as "a kind of huge spiderweb of the finest silken threads in the chamber of consciousness, and catching every air-borne particle in its tissue. . . . The province of art is all life, all feeling, all observation, all vision. . . . There is no impression of life, no manner of seeing it, to which the plan of the novelist may not offer a place. . . ."[9] Since one cannot restrict the "particles" which fall within the "spiderweb" of experience, the subject of homosexuality falls clearly within the province of the writer.

All art must explore "the mystery of the human being" and shed light on the entire spectrum of human experience. To the extent that a work of art presents vicarious experiences and viable alternatives, an artistic creation becomes an entity in itself, entirely separate from its creator. Therefore, it is legitimate to *interpret* autobiographical references within the work, but one can never *impose* those personal elements which occur entirely outside of the context of the work of art and allow them to impinge upon the creation itself.

Baldwin has neatly structured *Giovanni's Room* so that the basic action falls into four symmetrical episodes which relate David's experiences: The brief interlude with Joey and the longer relationship with Giovanni contrast sharply with the heterosexual scenes—the seduction of Sue and the sustained relationship with Hella. The homosexual experiences incite conflicting emotions of shame and satisfaction while the affairs with Sue and Hella promote feelings of acceptance and emptiness. The action of the novel is one of conflict between these forces as David is buffeted first by one and then the other. The resolution of the plot, in the *Bildungsroman* tradition, corresponds to David's attempts to come to grips with these irreconcilable options.

Like John Grimes, David has been utterly unsuccessful in establishing a warm, genuine relationship in his role as a heterosexual. His father had never recognized the need for "the merciful distance" conducive to a viable paternal relationship, and David, as a result, could not love him. They had never been able to "talk," to communicate with each other, and therefore David had acquired the habit of telling his father what he wanted to hear. An awareness of these dual, warring forces never dawned upon Ellen's consciousness, and she consistently substituted recriminations for patience and indulgence whenever her nephew came home drunk.

David vividly recalls for us the brief homosexual affair with Joey, and the intensity of this experience becomes clear immediately: "I feel in myself now a faint, dreadful stirring of what so over-whelmingly stirred in me then, great thirsty heat, and trembling, and tenderness so painful I thought my heart would burst. But out of this astounding, intolerable pain came joy; we gave each other joy that night. It seemed, then, that a lifetime would not be long enough for me to act with Joey the act of love" (14). And then suddenly the next morning, an unexplained fear, born of guilt, came over him, and we became aware for the first time of the magnitude of David's dilemma: "It was borne in on me: *But Joey is a boy*" (15).

The crux of this predicament is firmly rooted in the question of whether homosexuality is an illness from which one suffers or whether it is a choice that one makes. Eldridge Cleaver, in his at-tack on Baldwin, insists on the former interpretation: "I, for one, do not think homosexuality is the latest advance over heterosexuality on the scale of human evolution. Homosexuality is a sickness, just as are baby-rape or wanting to become the head of General Motors."[10] Baldwin, of course, insists that an individual has two options open to him and that one must be allowed to exercise his free choice in deciding between the two alternatives if he is to achieve his identi-ty. To deny an individual this selection is to reject the reality of these two choices: "This is one of the American myths. What always occurs to me is that people in other parts of the world have never had this peculiar kind of conflict. If you fall in love with a boy, you fall in love with a boy. The fact that Americans consider it a disease says more about them than it says about homosexuality. . . .

It's impossible to go through life assuming that you know who you're going to fall in love with. You don't."[11] But David has come to no such conclusion. Society in general insists on regarding homosexuality as a sexual deviation, and David has heretofore accepted this viewpoint unquestioningly. As a result he suffers feelings of guilt for having violated this social dictum and for the feelings of pleasure which he has derived from the experience. And so he futilely seeks release from his emotional quandary through a physical escape to France. He is totally unaware that the self from which he seeks to escape will, ultimately, be the identical being of his discovery.

## A.   *The Raging Storm*

It was in Paris that David met Hella Lincoln, and immediately they became attracted to each other. Each person seemed to per-

ceive the other as the source of an undefined, vague sense of fulfillment which the other needed. David, still clinging to conventional
morality, cherished Hella as his passport to social respectability. She
became the vehicle through which he could expiate the guilt that he
felt for his affair with Joey and confirm his masculinity in terms that
were acceptable to society: heterosexual love, marriage, and pater-
nity. Hella became the instrument of his freedom, his refuge from
the sexually ambivalent feelings from which he had sought release.
With her he could have a sense of normality, sanctioned by social
customs and mores. Hella, too, had come to Paris in search of self.
She had been kind in acknowledging David's casual offer of
marriage, but commitment seemed presently impossible for her.
She needed time and space to think, and Spain seemed the perfect
place for those deliberations.

Having lost his passport to social conformity, David's quandary
becomes even more intense when he meets Giovanni. Jacques advises David to "love him and let him love you. Do you think
anything else under heaven really matters?" (77). Yet the feelings of
shame which he had felt with Joey begin to close in on him. This
raging conflict of desire and reality versus shame and guilt reaches a
climax after David accompanies Giovanni to his room for the first
time and the door has been locked: "I thought, if I do not open the
door at once and get out of here, I am lost. But I knew I could not
open the door, I knew it was too late to do anything but moan. He
pulled me against him, putting himself into my arms as though he
were giving me himself to carry, and slowly pulled me down with
him into that bed. With everything in me screaming *No!* yet the
sum of me sighed *Yes*" (86 - 87). Latent desire became transformed
into actuality, and the "beast" in David had been resurrected, but
the voice of conformity continued to vie with his inner being.
Sometimes, in that room, he was filled with ecstasy and joy; at
others, as he reflected on his attachment to Giovanni, he experienced guilt and revulsion. At times he envisioned "Giovanni's
hands . . . which would have the power to crush me and make me
whole again" (117); at others, he longed for the means of an escape
to respectability.

It was on one of these latter occasions that he met Sue. She had
not been special; she had merely passed by during one of David's
hours of desperation. Hella was scheduled to return to Paris soon,
and he began to feel a pressing physical need for Sue in order to ex-
punge the memory of Giovanni from his consciousness and remove
all self-doubt regarding his masculinity. Reduced to this level, Sue's

seduction becomes an unpleasant, but necessary "job," the im-
morality of which David finds frightening. Sue, desperately in need
of the warmth and tenderness of human contact, extends her love,
only to be denied. David uses her in a desperate effort to achieve his
own selfish end, but he remains unsatisfied and unfulfilled.

Hella's return failed to quench the fire that raged in David. After
her Spanish interlude, she had decided to "be a woman" at all costs
and give herself to David in marriage. They made love in the morn-
ings, but it was never the same. The warmth of her body, the
tenderness of her caresses, all reminded him of the joy, the excite-
ment, the love that he had known in Giovanni's room. Hella had
made her decision, and now David must make his. He must reject
the myth of sexuality which had never ceased to haunt him, accept
the reality of his homosexual inclinations, and pursue his identity.
David can now make a confession which he dared not utter before:
"I loved him. I do not think I will ever love anyone like that again."
(148).

Hella and David have each chosen a path parallelling the other,
neither of which will converge, even in infinity. Having finally
accepted a life of social conformity, she returns to the narrow, con-
stricting confines of America in order to pursue the familial
relationships which she desires. David, having lost Giovanni, has
chosen to remain in the Parisian atmosphere of freedom. At last, the
raging storm within him has subsided, and he can now search for
peace and contentment.

### B.   *Freedom versus Conventionality*

Of particular significance in this novel is Baldwin's subtle
manipulation of imagery. Sue's apartment is described as
"cluttered," a term which clearly mirrors the myriad thoughts and
feelings that David experiences during their love-making. He has
become so saturated with these conflicting sensibilities that he is
unable to think rationally. He is convinced that through this affair
he can exorcise and purge the "beast" which has been aroused
within him.

The image of cleanliness is also of major importance. As Jacques
sits watching Giovanni in Guillaume's bar, David refuses his suggestion to invite Giovanni over to their table, and Jacques retorts sarcastically, " 'I was not suggesting that you jeopardize, even for a
moment, that'—he paused—'that *immaculate* manhood which is

your pride and joy' " (43). Cleanliness tends to suggest masculinity, and it is used consistently in reference to heterosexual relationships. When the landlady comes to inspect the villa which David had originally rented for Hella, she reminds him that " 'Everything was clean when you moved in' " (90). The guest bedroom, the kitchen, and the master bedroom which David and Hella used are all "clean and orderly," while the bathroom and David's bedroom are badly in need of cleaning. The images here reflect the half-clean, half-dirty state of David's mind and are used to heighten the homosexual-heterosexual conflict which, at this time, is still unresolved. Near the end of the novel, as David is about to leave, Giovanni angrily confronts him with his preoccupation to avoid the dirt and grime of reality: "You want to be *clean*. You think you came here covered with soap and you think you will go out covered with soap—and you do not want to *stink*, not even for five minutes, in the meantime" (187).

The image of dirt also abounds elsewhere in the novel. David remembers the episode with Joey as a "horrifying taint" which he likens to a "decomposing corpse." Later he describes the "garbage" in Giovanni's room, and he explains to him that their relationship is not socially acceptable: "People have very dirty words for—for this situation" (107). The moral condition is described as one of cleanliness as opposed to filth. And it is David who must decide between the socially sanctioned, sterile, and empty cleanliness to which he clings and a more satisfying life among the "dirt" and "garbage" of the streets.

The associations that are connected with these images are, of course, conventional ones. As David begins to move away from this orthodox posture, as he begins to honor his true feelings, these associations begin to reverse themselves. Hella becomes "stale," and he begins to "recoil" at her touch. Her lingerie, once "sweet," somehow becomes "unaesthetic and unclean," and David confronts himself with the reason for the change: " . . . the astonishment, the power, and the joy were gone, the peace was gone" (211).

The three major characters in the novel represent a kind of dynamic continuum in the Baldwin canon of morality. Hella Lincoln's acceptance of conventional social standards and her concern for moral propriety place her squarely to the right of the scale. The rebellious Giovanni, who attempts to find a moral center within himself, stands firmly at the left. Tottering precariously between these two extremes is David, who, while he rejects the communion

of the homosexuals, is unable to validate his membership among the
"conventionals." And it is the frustration born of this ambivalence
which functions as a pivotal point around which the action of the
story revolves.

Giovanni's Room is a novel which rises above the homosexual-
heterosexual framework of the action to consider the larger issue of
the failure of love. This failure, a consequence of the unexamined
life, has several manifestations in the novel: Sue has been grossly
exploited, Hella has suffered unnecessary pain and anguish, and
David, in denying his love, has precipitated Giovanni's death and
jeopardized his own potential for self-realization. David is not able
to rise to the challenge and provide the love which Giovanni urgent-
ly needs to support his very existence because he cannot face up to
reality and bear witness to the truth within himself. Since he is unable to examine his life, David deprives both Giovanni and himself
of the mutual satisfaction of love. It is not until David can
acknowledge this colossal failure that he gains the strength to abandon his illusions and strike out upon the high road of truth in search
of his identity.

## C.   Love: Search for Expression

Baldwin's probe into the complex question of sexuality is
developed more fully in Another Country.[12] Here, love, the virtue
of ultimate significance, takes no regard of provincial mores, ethnic
backgrounds, or national origins, and refuses confinement to the
narrow limitations symbolized by the conventional terms,
"heterosexuality" and "homosexuality." These barriers to communication are broken down—dissolved—and expressions of love in
the novel run the full gamut of possibility, according to the needs of
the individuals:

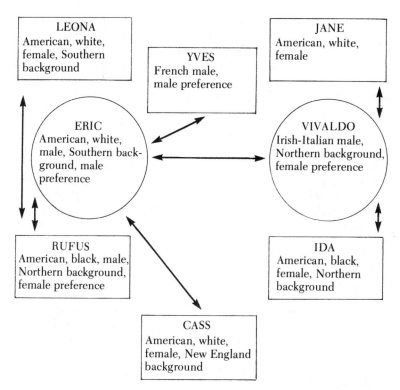

As this pattern indicates, Baldwin uses these fictional characters and their sexuality to fashion a symbolic unity out of the traditional racial, sectional, national, and sexual differences which have become obstacles to human communication. Further analysis of the design reveals that this unification takes place on ten different levels: (1) white male, black male (Rufus, Eric); (2) Irish-Italian male, black female (Vivaldo, Ida); (3) white male bisexuals (Eric, Yves); (4) white female, white male bisexual (Cass, Eric); (5) white male, white male bisexual (Vivaldo, Eric); (6) white male, white female (Vivaldo, Jane); (7) black male, white female (Rufus, Leona); (8) American male, French male (Eric, Yves); (9) Northern female, Southern male (Cass, Eric); (10) Northern male, Southern female (Rufus, Leona). Eric and Vivaldo seem to function as pivots for these relationships, since Eric is active in four of the patterns, while Vivaldo is involved in three.

In a technical sense, among Baldwin's major male characters, there are no homosexuals or heterosexuals because, for him, these labels are nonexistent. This accounts for the fact that Rufus, Vivaldo, and Eric all have varying degrees of bisexual inclinations. The same pattern may also be traced in *Giovanni's Room*. In the middle of the novel we learn that Giovanni had a wife and a mistress, and although his current interests are masculine, he acknowledges the possibility of future female relationships. In the span of the novel, David participates in affairs with Joey, Hella, Giovanni, and Sue. However, in denying the orthodox categories of sexuality, Baldwin never leaves his men without the duality of sexual experience necessary to make the choice concerning the vehicle by which they will express their love. He seems to visualize only a hairline between the two expressions, so that once a character has declared his preference, he retains inherently an implicit freedom to exercise the alternative to his choice, according to need. It is this same thin line which prompts Cass to ignore Eric's confession of his affair with Yves and allow him to make love to her.

The entire question of choice becomes apparent throughout *Another Country*. Vivaldo rejects the sexual advances made by his barroom acquaintance, Harold, although he willingly makes love with Eric. Rufus, too, accepts Eric, but he cannot degrade himself to be bought for the price of a sandwich by the man in the bar. By the end of the novel, Vivaldo elects to remain with Ida, and Eric, apparently, has decided to continue his relationship with Yves. Yet both of these individuals are able to make this choice only after a variety of sexual experiences and considerable agonizing and introspective analysis.

## D.  *Love: Failure and Frustration*

The candid depiction of sex which frequently offends the puritan sensibilities of the reader exists as a vehicle through which Baldwin explores the failure of love in our society. Near the beginning of the novel, Rufus vividly recalls the last time he played in a new Harlem nightclub. A young saxophone player had captured the spotlight. Rufus *watched* the boy as he took command of the instrument, and he *heard* the youth as he screamed a frantic question which seemed to pierce every nerve and stimulate the very fiber of his being: "*Do you love me? Do you love me?* And again, *Do you love me? Do you love me? Do you love me?*" (13). Rufus is able to identify with the mood of desperation because he, too, longs to ask this question, to cry aloud a supplication that someone will understand his crucial need to receive love and save him from destruction. It is this same question, this same cry of anguish and pain from which all of Baldwin's characters are seeking relief.

Each of the major characters is suffering from a most profound isolation: estrangement from the past. Cass, in choosing to marry the son of a Polish carpenter, has been condemned to live in social exile from her aristocratic New England family; and Richard, in turn, has exchanged his Polish ancestry for the dubious fame and recognition which he achieves as a writer. Rufus becomes estranged from his family because of his licentious life style and his white mistress, Leona. Ida earns the contempt of her parents because she dares to become involved with a white sexual partner. Vivaldo's isolation from his alcoholic father and his relationship with Ida make him the black sheep of the family. Eric has been banished for his youthful, illicit intimacies with his black Alabama friend, LeRoy; and Yves has long since despised his mother, who seemed to enjoy bargaining her favors with the German soldiers. But the cross of alienation becomes too heavy for these people to bear, and they cry out in agony as they search for the redeeming power of love.

Baldwin makes us aware, from the very beginning of the novel, of the ominous forces which conspire to oppress and kill, while Rufus strives to avoid the "murderous," crushing weight of New York, which becomes symbolic of the cunning, cruel, and merciless white-oriented society. And he struggles amid feelings of frustration and hostility, waging what he senses to be a losing battle with the Establishment for survival: "You got to fight with the landlord because the landlord's *white!* You got to fight with the elevator boy because the motherfucker's *white.* Any bum on the Bowery can shit all over you because maybe he can't hear, can't see, can't walk, can't fuck—but he's *white!* (62)." Thus, the search for love and the struggle for survival give rise to the haunting question, "Do you love me?"

Ironically, it is a Southern white girl who dares to answer Rufus's call. Leona, too, is in search of love. She had known pain and suffering and had escaped these ordeals to make a new life in the North. Leona offers her love unselfishly as a means of extricating Rufus from the prison of his hatred, but he cannot reciprocate that love. Hatred, fear, anguish, and frustration have been etched indelibly upon his brain, and he can only use Leona as he has been ill used by a white society. Symbolic of that society, she becomes the object of his scorn, contempt, humiliation, and abuse. Unable to recognize Leona's love, Rufus can only view her motive for remaining his mistress from a purely physical point of view: sexual gratification. He cannot surmount the indestructible barriers erected by centuries of racial inhumanity in order to accept Leona's love for him and to return that love. His great need, he confides to Vivaldo, is that "I want the chick to love me. I want to make her love me. I want to be loved. . . . How do you *make* it happen? . . . What do you *do*?" (63). Nevertheless, Leona is persistent in her futile, pathetic efforts to overcome those barriers—those overwhelming obstacles to communication, to love and self-realization. She tries desperately, though ineffectually, to fathom the black American experience and to regard Rufus with compassion and understanding: " 'I love him', she said helplessly, 'I love him, I can't help it. No matter what he does to me. He's just lost and he beats me because he can't find nothing else to hit' " (55).

Rufus's white friend, Vivaldo Moore, might also have served as the instrument of his salvation. But Vivaldo could not bear to face Rufus's reality because it reminded him of his own past which had long been buried among the ruins of his subconscious. Consequently, it is not until after Rufus's death that Vivaldo is able to make the connection between Rufus's suffering and his own. Enroute to the funeral, he recalls for Cass his initial reaction to the neighborhood where his friend's parents were living: " 'I walked through that block and I walked in that house and it all seemed—I don't know—familiar.' He turned his pale, troubled face toward her but she felt that he was staring at the high, hard wall which stood between himself and the past" (98). Somehow the vague feeling of guilt for the part that he played in Rufus's death had begun to work its way into his consciousness. But it is not until after his brief relationship with Eric that he is able to implicate himself in Rufus's death. Vivaldo recalls sleeping with Rufus the night before his death, and he gains the courage to articulate that guilt which remains pent up inside of him: "I guess I still wonder, what would have happened if I'd taken him in my arms, if I'd held him, if I hadn't been—afraid. . . . But, oh, Lord, when he died, I thought that maybe I could have saved him, if I'd just reached out that quarter of an inch between us on that bed, and held him" (289). Vivaldo cannot cope with the problems which Rufus encounters in his world; instead, he prefers to wrestle with the manipulable fates of the characters in his unpublished novel.

Vivaldo stands as a pivotal character in the novel because of his dual function as Rufus's friend and Ida's lover. As Vivaldo becomes aware of Ida's involvement with television producer Steve Ellis, once again he is in a position to save. Just as he might have redeemed Rufus's life, Vivaldo is faced with the choice of rescuing Ida. He alone is able to offer her the love necessary to preserve her dignity and self-respect. But, as Ida comments, he ". . . didn't want to know what was happening to me" (356) because he was afraid of coming to grips with reality.

Like Vivaldo, Richard Silenski also seeks to escape his heritage in pursuit of the American Dream. Having entered the professional world, Richard dreams not of self-fulfillment but of self-achievement. His visions become delusions of social power and prestige rather than hopes for inner satisfaction and peace. Each aspiration becomes the means of scaling the mountain and joining the mainstream of society. The long struggle up has earned for him many badges of conformity: a plush apartment, a wife of aristocratic ancestry, two fine boys, and the publication of his first novel. He is so obsessed with these trappings of success that he becomes oblivious to Cass's urgent need to be loved. And while Cass enjoys these things, she is unable to suppress her yearnings for self-fulfillment. She turns away from Richard and accepts Eric as her lover in the hope that "perhaps each could teach the other, concerning love, what neither now knew . . ." (246). Cass's great yearning was "to be a woman," and she had been denied the realization of that hope.

Cass entertains no delusions about the permanence of her relationship with Eric. From the very beginning he had told her of his affair with Yves, and she was aware of the "transient bed" upon which she offered herself to him. She knew that Eric's lover would reclaim him and that Richard, eventually, would discover her infidelity. And then that day arrived. Richard had suspected Vivaldo, only to have Cass reveal the name of Eric. But why Eric? Why Eric? he asked. Immediately, Cass responded, "He has something—something I needed very badly. . . . A sense of himself" (314-315). It is precisely this self-realization that Richard so woefully lacks.

## E. *Another Dream, Another Country*

Baldwin makes a perceptive though subtle observation on the perverted values of our society in contrasting the fates of Richard

Silenski and Rufus Scott. Both men are members of minority groups, both have experienced the demoralizing effects of racial prejudice, and both are aspiring artists. Each man is required by society to compromise his values—a compromise which results in fame for Richard and death for Rufus. The perennial racist argument, applied to this situation, is that Rufus could have "pulled himself up by his bootstraps" and succeeded just as Richard did. Ambition, it is argued, has no regard for race. Yet it would seem that this is a gross oversimplification of the problem, as Baldwin explains in his discussion of the concept of "rising expectations":
". . . it is perfectly true that the idea of rising expectations is part of the American experience: You leave the famine-ridden farm in Ireland, you come to America, you fit into the American scene, you rise, you become part of a new social structure. But that is only the European immigrants' experience. It is not the Black experience. . . . The black experience is entirely different. You find yourself in a slum and you realize at a certain point that no amount of labor, no amount of hard work, no amount of soap is going to get you out of that slum."[13]

This is precisely the dilemma that faced Rufus Scott, black American from the ghetto of Harlem, and he becomes symbolic of the countless thousands of other black youth, lacking the hope of "rising expectations," who succumb to the insidious forces perpetuated by the white social order. Survival depends upon the black man's recognition that "the standards by which the country lives are not for him, and he knows that by the time he starts pledging allegiance to the flag. . . . Somehow you have to operate outside the system and beat these people at their own game."[14] Those who, like Rufus, are unsuccessful in performing this Herculean task are not to blame. The responsibility, the guilt for these failures must rest where it belongs. And neither soap nor soapbox rhetoric can absolve this society of its sinister complicity in these deeds.

Shortly before his death, Rufus begins to listen to the whistle of the riverboats, and he thinks,". . . wouldn't it be nice to get on a boat again and go someplace away from all these nowhere people, where a man could be treated like a man" (62). Rufus longs for another country where his dream of love can reach fruition. But neither he nor any of the other major characters is ever able to enter that country.

In the final scenes of the novel, the movement of the characters from innocence to experience becomes evident. Vivaldo, having failed both Ida and Rufus, gains the courage to involve himself in another individual's emotions and experiences. As a result, he is able to put aside his fantasies about Ida's life, accept her confession of infidelity, and honor the tender feelings for her which yet remain. Cass discovers that the image of Richard which she has fashioned is a false one. She begins to realize, finally, that she has loved her husband as a child and that her true personality has been sublimated to Richard's needs. Eric matures to the extent that he begins to understand that frustration and anguish are vital components of human nature. It is this awareness that gives him the strength to rise and achieve a final acceptance of his bisexuality. All of these characters are moving "toward Bethlehem," as the title of Book Three suggests. Having rejected traditional barriers of family, race, country, religion, and sex, they are progressing toward a discovery of their own "moral centers" which, ultimately, hold the promise of a new and total understanding of themselves.

### III  Reaching for Self: Frustration and Accommodation

*Tell Me How Long the Train's Been Gone,*[15] Baldwin's fourth novel, is the story of the Proudhammer brothers—Caleb and Leo—and their efforts to deal with the facts of life in the ghetto environment into which they were born: the insolent landlord; the heatless, rat-infested, dilapidated apartment; the perennial grocery bill; and the brutal, inhumane defenders of the power structure, the police. But it is also the story of these brothers' determined efforts to transcend these depressing, frustrating, murderous elements and launch the quest for self.

By the time Caleb Proudhammer reached the age of seventeen, he had become cynical about the entire power structure—both secular and divine. He had become skeptical of God, who, through inability or indifference, had allowed the agents of law and order to whip black heads with impunity. This attitude is manifested when the police detain Caleb and little Leo on the street for a brief frisking and then decide to release them: "Thanks, you white cocksucking dog-shit miserable white motherfuckers. Thanks, all you scum-bag Christians. . . . Thanks, good Jesus Christ. Thanks for letting us go home. I mean, I know you didn't have to do it. You *could* have let us just get our brains beat out. Remind me to put a extra large nickel in the plate next Sunday . . ." (45). Caleb has decided that he has "never met a good [white man]," and this contempt is heightened by the treatment he receives from the power structure when he is later implicated by his friends in a store robbery. In spite of his innocence, Caleb spends four years on a Southern prison farm under intolerable conditions. When he finally returns to Harlem after the terror of unspeakable horrors, his spirit has been broken, but the storm of bitterness and hostility continues to rage within his breast. Soon Caleb leaves for the shipyards of California, and then, after having run afoul of the law there, he joins the army.

Near the opening of Book III there is a casual reference to Caleb's wife and children, and a few pages later Baldwin presents us with a new Caleb who had been wounded in the European theater, found the Lord, returned to New York, and joined The New Dispensation House of God (281). Here, however, the credibility of the novel becomes questionable because this very complex change in Caleb's character is summarized; we cannot see the transformation through the plot development. We have no way of accounting for this change, although Caleb's recollection of his army experiences for Leo later at The Island restaurant seems to be an effort in this direction: Caleb's buddy, Frederick, had stolen his girlfriend, Pia, and Caleb had vowed revenge. But before he could reach Frederick in the field, a sniper shot rang out, and Frederick fell mortally wounded, thinking that Caleb had got his revenge. Caleb reflects that, *immediately*, upon the battlefield, "I struggled up to my knees. I knew, I knew for the first time that there was a God somewhere. I knew that only God could save me, save us, not from death, but from that other death, that darkness and death of the spirit which had created this hell. . . . I understood for the first time the power and the beauty of the love of God" (309-310). The instantaneous nature of Caleb's conversion here is perfectly plausible. But one does question the immediacy of the complete understanding attendant to that conversion, especially in light of the earlier monologue which clearly reflects contempt and mockery for a white God and a white establishment. As a result, the reader is left, in spite of the revelation of Caleb's romantic triangle, without a full justification for the new man who emerges.

The original Caleb might easily have joined Leo's friend Christopher in the Black Power call for arms. But Baldwin substitutes, instead of a potential revolutionary, a clean-cut exponent of conventionality with all of the traditional trappings: a wife, two children, a home, a chauffeur's job, and an assistant pastorship on the side. Caleb has, in effect, made his truce with reality. Unable to escape the ghetto, he insulates himself against the abuses and injustices suffered by blacks and takes refuge in relgion.

## A. *Reality and Verisimilitude*

In his review of *Tell Me*, Irving Howe takes Baldwin to task for a "compulsive use of obscenity." Howe brushes aside as "incompetent" the suggestion that the characters' speech is realistic because "no novelist . . . can avoid the need to compress and stylize his dialogue. . . ." Instead, he accuses Baldwin of appealing to the *Zeitgeist*.[16] If I am correct in assuming that Caleb's speech after the cop-frisking is typical of the street language to which Howe objects, it would seem that the criticism is unwarranted. Caleb Proudhammer, we must remember, has been bred in an atmosphere of frustration and despair. He has come to resent all authority which, he has concluded, is in conspiracy to destroy the spirit and the dignity of the black man at the price of the destruction of the physical body, if necessary. Having rejected the formal education designed for him by society, he has become educated in the street where he has learned the strategy necessary to survive the pistol butt and the billy club of the police. His frustrations, therefore, are communicated through the only language that he has at his command. And that is the language of the street. If it is true, as Howe suggests, that Baldwin is reacting to his compulsive need to reveal himself as "a very up-to-the-minute swinger, a real tough guy, . . .," then it seems equally certain that he displays an abiding concern for the achievement of verisimilitude which emantes from the complexity of his own experiences in the Harlem ghetto. Hence, it would seem that if this authenticity has been accomplished at the expense of our straitlacedness, the end justifies the means which Baldwin employs.

Leo Proudhammer experiences his first encounter with the law while he and Caleb are on their way home from the subway. We have noted Caleb's reaction to this incident, and it would be profitable to consider Leo's impressions here: " . . . I watched the white faces. I memorized the eyes, the contemptuous eyes. I wished that I were God" (45). Interestingly enough, as the two boys discuss the experience, suddenly Leo begins to question Caleb, " . . . Are white people—*people*? People like us?" Caleb responds, "All I can tell you Leo, is—well *they* don't think they are" (46). Again Howe objects to the dialogue, this time on the grounds of plausibility. Ten-year-old Leo, he observes, is still ". . . a little boy, still rather innocent and strongly protected by his family. Can we then believe that at this frightening moment he would wish he were God? I greatly doubt it. . . ." And if we accept the fact that Leo hates

God, Howe continues, " . . . who can suppose that a boy sophisticated enough to have learned to 'hate God' can a few pages later be innocent enough to wonder whether whites are 'people'?"[17]

What Howe fails to recognize here is that we are dealing not with a white, poverty-stricken child, but with a black ten-year-old boy growing up in Harlem. And innocence is notoriously short-lived in the ghetto where one is forced early to barter his naïveté for the sophistication and the strategies that facilitate survival. The typical black ghetto offspring, tragically, must suffer an abbreviated childhood and learn the lessons of the street. These lessons become vital, urgent experiences from which no black family can protect its young. Children learn early that their parents are powerless within the white social structure which surrounds them. These parents are unable to protect their children because they themselves are victims of the legal and social systems. Consequently, children are quick to realize that the police are paid to brutalize and humiliate black people by those who hold the balance of power in the community. Caleb explains this situation to Leo, and the young boy reflects, "It seemed, now, that I had always known it, though I had never been able to say it. But I do not understand it" (46). Circumstances in the ghetto have forced Leo to intuit these realities and to act in accordance with them, although he cannot yet understand why they are so. Aware of the powerlessness of black mortals, he appeals to God. And he hates God because He represents the Supreme Power who seems too indifferent to protect him from the inhumanity of the white community.

It is an incontestable fact that we tend to measure humanity exclusively by those specimens most like ourselves. Leo has experienced humanity in the ghetto, and he begins to wonder how it is possible that human beings can terrorize and kill other human beings in the name of justice, law, and order. Can they be human beings as he knows them within his frame of reference? This is a legitimate query—perhaps not for the average white ten-year-old—but certainly well within the range of the ghetto child's sensibilities. Accordingly, it would be mystifying indeed if Leo had not had grave difficulty in resolving this dichotomy.

B. *The Denial of Love: A New Story?*

Baldwin traces Leo's development through the dilapidated tenements of Paradise Alley, the frustrations of the Actors' Means

Workshop, and the affair with the white actress, Barbara King. Leo
had met Barbara in Paradise Alley, and, brushing aside Leo's admission of bisexuality, she had declared her love for him during the
summer workshop. Baldwin is at his best here as he portrays the injustices and indignities that Leo and Barbara are forced to suffer.
Here he introduces the *lietmotif* of the failure of love between these
two people. Like Vivaldo and Ida in *Another Country*, Barbara and
Leo have been ostracized by their families and by society as well.
Having been deprived of this stability, these lovers find themselves
without the security and support necessary to sustain their
relationship. And their suffering becomes a wretched, lonely misery. Barbara and Leo are compelled, therefore, to accept the denial
of love which results from an inescapable, impenetrable hostility
born of white prejudice: "Some nights, the entire town was in the
house with us. . . . I knew, at the very bottom of my heart that we
could not succeed. Of all the fears there are, perhaps the fear of
physical pain and destruction is the most devastating. . . . I didn't
want all my teeth knocked out, didn't want my nose smashed, my
eyes blinded, didn't want my skull caved in. . . . Fear and love
cannot long remain in the same bed together" (269).

There were the ugly taunts, the epithets, the violence,
perpetrated by young and old alike, which conspired to incite terror
and instill those fears with which love could not contend. And there
were the parents on either side who had become subscribers to the
racist concept of miscegenation. There could be no way of recon-
ciling these dichotomies; hence, fear became the instrument by
which the bigoted townspeople were able to stifle all human communication. In spite of their love, the future held no possibilities;
the relationship had been doomed from the beginning. Love, Leo
discovered, was not enough; commitment was also essential, but he
could not allow himself that luxury: "The most subtle and perhaps
the most deadly alienation is that which is produced by the fear of
being alienated. Because I was certain that Barbara could not stay
with me, I dared not be committed to Barbara. This fear obscured a
great many fears, but it obscured, above all, the question of whether
or not I wished to be committed to Barbara, or to anyone else, and it
hid the question of whether or not I was capable of commitment . . ." (274). Like the two lovers in the scene which Leo
and Barbara perform in the workshop, they, too, are helplessly and
innocently trapped. Barbara and Leo had been called upon by
society to deny themselves the traditional security and stability of a

home and family without hostility and resentment. And it was inevitable that they should decide, ultimately, upon the impossibility
of learning to live in that trap that society had so carefully fashioned.

The remainder of Leo's struggle to reach the top—the singing-
waiter job at The Island, the ignominious bit parts, and finally the
big break in the experimental theater production of *The Corn Is
Green*—are all sketchily summarized. Baldwin might have been
more effective here had he given a sharper focus and a more detailed view of the action by dispensing with some of the longer, less
significant cocktail parties and *tete à tetes*.

Another shortcoming in *Tell Me*, Calvin Hernton argues, is its
lack of depth or dimension. In discussing the merits of the novel, he
contends that "A writer may write about the same things involving
the same elements for as long as he lives. . . . But each time there
should be a new dimension, a new depth, a new *something;* the
same people and the same general problems, all right, but the
nature of the specific problem must somehow emerge as a
qualitatively new or different story."[18] And indeed, as we look back
on Baldwin's concerns in the three previous novels, we find many
duplications that tend to give Hernton's charge a certain validity:
(1) bisexual relationships sustained by male characters (*Giovanni's
Room, Another Country*); (2) inability of males to identify with
fathers (*Go Tell, Giovanni's Room, Another Country*); (3) alienation
from family (*Go Tell, Giovanni's Room, Another Country*); (4) im-
prisonment of innocent blacks due to racial prejudice (*Go Tell*); (5)
difficulties involved in black-white heterosexual relationships
(*Another Country*); (6) inhumane treatment of blacks by police (*Go
Tell*). Where, then, one might ask, is the new "depth" or "dimension"? A careful consideration of the love affair between Leo and
Black Christopher seems to reveal, at the end of the novel, that Leo
has begun to analyze his own posture as a "fat cat." He has achieved "success" as an actor, and, resultingly, he has become alienated
from the grass roots. It is Christopher who acts as a catalyst in
bringing about this epiphany. How can the social trap constructed
by racial myth be sprung for the benefit of posterity? What can be
done to help Christopher, symbol of black youth, in his efforts to
avoid the interminable plight of "going under the feet of horses?"
Leo ponders these questions, and the result of the deliberations is
clear: He can only relieve himself of the "terrible weight on my
heart" (370) by aligning himself with the new revolutionary movement which Christopher represents.

## IV *Love: Achievement and Fruition*

The full range and scope of the Baldwin artistic continuum becomes even more apparent in the most recent novel, *If Beale Street Could Talk*.[19] For it is here that we witness the magnificent rhythm of the artistic pendulum in its graceful, deliberate sway to and fro. It swings to form a coherent bridge between past and present to remind us of the hypocrisies inherent in the American system of justice. It sweeps into the past to reiterate the woeful lack of humanitarianism, love, and compassion in a Christianity whose members are unable to transcend such doctrinal and ceremonial minutiae as regular church attendance and the physical manifestations of religious fervor. But more importantly, the pendulum also swings into the present in a new dimensional thrust which seems to provide the elements, as Hernton describes them, of "a qualitatively new or different story." Throughout the first four novels, Baldwin's characters grope hopelessly for the realization of love. But *If Beale Street* represents a consummation, an achievement, for it is here that love is fulfilled.

Baldwin's presentation of the issue of judicial miscarriage is typical of his earlier artistry, with all the elements of blatant injustice: the racist policeman who needs a black rape suspect, the black youth who is conveniently arrested and sent to jail without bond, and the deliberate, calculated grinding of the wheels of "justice" as they move slowly but inexorably toward the conviction of an innocent black victim. It is ironic that the fundamental American principle of presumption of innocence is swiftly and irrevocably suspended while Fonny's family is forced to establish his innocence. They realize the necessity for assuming the awesome burden of proof, and they accept that responsibility unflinchingly, as Ernestine observes: "We have to disprove the state's case. There's no point in saying that we have to make *them* prove it, because, as far as they're concerned, the accusation *is* the proof . . ." (119). The cherished ideal of equality under the law which protects can also be used to condemn. Power drives morality the full distance to obscure obsolescence, and veracity dons the garb of relativity and expedience, to be manipulated by the "keepers of the keys and seals" at will. Fonny's lawyer, Hayward, succinctly assesses this hypocrisy as he testifies to this ineffectuality of the American system of justice: "The truth of a case doesn't matter. What matters is—who wins" (93). Questions of innocence and guilt become moot issues in a contest which requires a clever manipulation of the facts. And the lives of men caught in the net of justice hang in the balance.

Baldwin deliberately and systematically sorts his characters into two factions—Christians and non-Christians—and he reverses the traditional distinctions that we normally associate with each group. The leader of the religious fanatics, Alice Hunt, is a proud, vain matriarch whose appreciation of the meticulous details of religious ceremony is rivalled only by her love of fine clothes and her ostentatious display of religious fervor. Craving admiration, she is an avid, sanctimonious church-goer who is intent upon displaying her religious talents on the most auspicious occasions. This image comes to us through Tish's recollection of a Sunday morning service where Mrs. Hunt competes with an adversary for the attention of the congregation: "Now I began to watch another sister, seated on the other side of Fonny, darker and plainer than Mrs. Hunt but just as well-dressed, who was throwing up her hands and crying, Holy! Holy! Bless your name, Jesus! And Mrs. Hunt started crying out and seemed to be answering her: it was like they were trying to out-do each other . . ."(25).

Rejecting this sacrilegious spectacle, Fonny and Tish, like Baldwin himself, disassociate themselves from the church. But Mrs. Hunt is supported in the starring role by her sexually promiscuous daughters, Sheila and Adrienne. The girls are well-dressed and, like their supercilious mother, they are victims of the fair-skin syndrome. Both mother and daughters have acquired a religion of convenience which unites them in their merciless indifference to Fonny's fate.

Into the non-Christian camp, Baldwin has placed the Rivers family—Tish, Ernestine, Sharon, and Joe—and the Hunt men, Fonny and Frank. Together these characters make up a family unit, whose ultimate effectiveness must be measured by the criterion set forth by Grier and Cobbs: " . . . a family is a functional unit designed for one primary purpose—the protection of the young; and while it serves other vital social purposes, none is more important than the function of *protection*."[20] Unlike any other family within the entire range of Baldwin's fiction, this family has power because its members have banded together and pooled their meager financial resources in a cohesive, concerted effort to defeat the Establishment which has harassed, humiliated, abused, jailed, beaten, robbed, killed, and raped black people since the acceptance of slavery as

a way of life in this country. They have power because they are united by their sympathy and compassion for humanity, by their
mutual love and respect, by their strong, clannish ties, and by their
unyielding determination to free Fonny and protect his heirs
forever from the enslaving institutions of our capitalistic society.

It is ironic indeed that as Fonny struggles desperately, clinging to
the slender thread of life, the Hunt women are unable to respond.
Theirs is a fantasy world of sham and hypocrisy, devoid of all sub-
stance, separated by the high wall of illusion from the practical
realities of daily existence. They have been brainwashed to the extent that they have accepted unequivocally the white myth that the
black man is "incorrigible" and "worthless." Misguided by the
perverted zeal of white supremacy, they provide evidence against
their son and brother.

Yet the non-Christian family becomes the divine instrument
through which love is fulfilled. The peace that reigns in the Rivers'
household contrasts sharply with the strife of the Hunts, and
enhances the image of the family as the final hope of a loveless people. In its efforts to protect Tish's baby, the family becomes the
protector of life and the source of hope and inspiration, as opposed
to the decadence and sterility of Christianity.

The story presented in *If Beale Street* is indeed a love story,
though not in the traditional sense. On one level, we have Eros as a
*personal* force. It is the physical and emotional response that leads
to the individual self-realization of two people, Fonny and Tish.
However, the love story, when viewed from this perspective, is
merely peripheral. Beyond these confines of individuality lies a
communal love. The feelings of affection and mutual concern
shared by the members of the family are directed not toward individual self-fulfillment, but toward a familial love which, by the
nature of its collectivism, transcends the individual component of
the emotion in order to reveal a vaster, more compelling aspect of
love.

The family has always been a significant factor in Baldwin's
novels. John's failure to identify with his stepfather in *Go Tell* and
his feelings of alienation from the family unit have a very definite
impact on his homosexual tendency. It is this same lack of genuine
communication among family members and the specific rejection of
the male parent that results in the bisexual characteristics that
dominate the lives of David (*Giovanni's Room*), Rufus, Vivaldo, and

Eric (*Another Country*), and Leo (*Tell Me*). But in contrast to these earlier novels, not only does the family unit in *If Beale Street* function as a protective shield for Fonny, but it also exerts a dominant influence on his sexuality. From the very beginning of the novel we are aware that Fonny idealizes Frank, and he is quick to understand that the elder Hunt has gained the strength to endure the unbearable life with Fonny's mother solely through the father's immeasurable love for his son. And, unlike the gamut of male characters that dominate Baldwin's previous novels, Fonny enjoys a mutual and abiding love for his "protective" family. Because of the peace and security which this family affords him, Fonny is able to ward off the homosexual advances made toward him during his penal confinement. He cherishes the memories of his intimacies with Tish, and he yearns to return to his heterosexual role as husband and lover. Consistent with this point of view, Baldwin's depiction of the heterosexual relationship suggests a reversal of the earlier portrayals in *Go Tell*. Instead, the two brief episodes that Tish summons from among her memories of Fonny are rendered with a passion and a tenderness which flow from the love that these young people share. The act of copulation becomes a movement toward life; it becomes a creative act which ultimately celebrates the continuity of the human race.

The ending of the novel represents a victory in several respects. The black family has banded together, and it has been successful in its efforts to thwart the advance of the sinister social forces that seek to humiliate and to enslave. The freedom of Tish's baby, the link between present and future generations, has been assured. Although he continues to dwell in a legal limbo, Fonny has been released from prison, and he has been united with Tish and the baby. Love and freedom have triumphed in the skirmish, but the battle continues to rage all around us.

In Baldwin's novels, love is often extended, frequently denied, seldom fulfilled. As reflections of our contemporary American society, the novels stand as forthright indictments of the intolerable conditions that we have accepted unquestioningly as a way of life. Injustices upon injustices have been perpetrated and imposed upon innocent heads until the human psyche—black and white alike—has become perverted and corrupt. In this atmosphere love cannot survive. We have substituted illusion for reality and cruelty and indifference for love, and our values have become hollow and meaningless. Moments of love, Baldwin seems to say, are precious, rare occasions to be cherished, and we must create an atmosphere where they can survive and flourish. We must find the means of reestablishing a genuine concern for the fate of our brothers. We must discover that "other country" within the depths of ourselves so that love can again become a possibility in our lives.

# CHAPTER 4

# *The Darkness Within*

## I  *The Common Chord*

THERE has always been a need for the unrestrained expression of black culture in American literature—the hope and despair, courage and fear, satisfaction and frustration, joy and sorrow felt by black people with concern neither for the values of white society nor for the restrictions that it seeks to impose upon the black artist. Indeed, there is no reason why the black artist should espouse white values, nor should he desire to incorporate those values in his writings.

As the artist exercises this unlimited freedom to explore the black soul, the mosaic pattern of a black world view emerges. We would not, of course, expect this view to coincide with the white world view any more than it would be reasonable to assume that Orientalism would duplicate the world view of the Occident. Yet, in any world view—black, white, Oriental, or Occidental—in a very basic sense, we can recognize certain *inherent* values of a universal nature. Listed among these yearnings and strivings are freedom from oppression, the discovery of self-identity, a profound pride in one's racial origins, a deep and abiding respect for one's culture, and a fervent belief in posterity as a means of propagating the heritage of the past and pointing toward new directions for the future.

In a real sense, then, the major problem of the black dramatist is identical to that of the black novelist: He must be able to effect the transmutation of his experience into the complex embodiment of a work of literary art. He must never *deny* the experiences of his culture, but he must be able to *interpret* his own cultural background in terms of universality, in terms of those experiences that strike a common chord of understanding and appreciation among humankind. He must present a work that radiates a certain limitlessness through the presentation of ideas, issues, and conflicts which are not bound by the ethnic, social, or even cultural milieu out of which they have come.

The term "universality," then, refers to those overlapping cultural elements that are recognizable and meaningful to peoples of differing ethnic, social, and cultural. backgrounds. The black dramatist (or novelist, for that matter) must never abandon or underestimate the legitimacy of his own experiences. Instead, he must reaffirm those experiences within the broader context of human worth and values. He must accept the role of luminary which, according to Baldwin, is the *raison d'etre* of the artist in society: ". . . the conquest of the physical world is not man's only duty. He is also enjoined to conquer the great wilderness of himself. The precise role of the artist, then, is to illuminate that darkness, blaze roads through that vast forest, so that we will not, in all our doing, lose sight of its purpose, which is, after all, to make the world a more human dwelling place." [1]

Let us consider Baldwin's plays from this perspective. The questions for which we shall seek answers are these: How do Baldwin's dramas, in fact, project beyond the world of protest and racism into the sanctuary of art? What are the dramatic techniques that he uses in his painstaking efforts to depict black life and culture and reveal the inherent universal values which emerge from the portraits he has drawn? What is there of human value in the ideas of these dramas? What illumination is shed on the "great wilderness of self" as man gropes amid the darkness in quest of self-identity and fulfillment?

## II  *Confusion and Conflict*

Sometimes the phrase "religious drama" is applied by Baldwin's critics to his first dramatic effort, *The Amen Corner*.[2] This meaningless and inappropriate epithet reflects a superficial grasp of the more significant aspects of the drama. It is a categorization which precisely points up the reason many critics are unable to analyze the broader philosophical aspects that dominate the play. They cannot view the *whole* drama of conflict because religion, the *part*, has obscured their view. Perhaps also, the critics have fallen victim to the idea that the black man's world is a sphere of religious and racial consciousness, and therefore it is expected that the theme of religion should dominate his writings in the instances where race has failed to prevail. I suggest that *Amen* is not a "religious drama" but rather a drama of interpersonal conflict, set against the background of a storefront Holy Roller church in Harlem. Only if we view the drama from this perspective can we discover the deeper human emotions and involvements with which the playwright is concerned.

Near the opening of *The Amen Corner* it becomes obvious that Margaret Alexander, the church's pastor, has fled the world of reality to take refuge—not in religion—but in illusion and self-deception. We find her in the midst of a homiletic rejoinder to the congregation's concepts of religion: "Some of you say, 'Ain't no harm in reading the funny papers.' But children, *yes*, there's harm in it. While you reading them funny papers, your mind ain't on the Lord. And if your mind ain't stayed on Him, every hour of the day, Satan's going to cause you to fall. Amen! Some of you say, 'Ain't no harm in me working for a liquor company. I ain't going to be drinking the liquor, I'm just going to be driving the truck!' But a saint ain't got no business delivering liquor to folks all day . . ." (9).

This admonition raises the ancient, yet valid question of whether or not some objects can be considered intrinsically good or evil apart from their social context. Obviously, Margaret's response would be affirmative. But illusion suggests confusion, and even Margaret is not always consistent in her attitude. When she is questioned about the "worldliness" of the drums and trumpets that the Philadelphia church members plan to bring to New York, she tells Sister Rice that "the evil is in what folks do with [the drum or trumpet] and what it leads them to. Ain't no harm in praising the Lord with anything you get in your hands" (53).

But that "anything" does not include a liquor truck. Sister Boxer recognizes this incongruity and continues her challenge: "Well, ain't a truck a *thing*? And if it's all right to blow a trumpet in church, why ain't it all right for Joel to drive that truck, so he can contribute a little more to the house of God?" (54). Margaret replies simply that there is "all the difference in the world." She can clearly see that a musical instrument has no intrinsic moral significance, but she fails to regard the liquor truck in that same light.

Another theme in the play concerns the perversion of one of the basic concepts of Christianity: humanitarianism. The foundation of Christian doctrine rests on the compassion and sympathy of one human being for another—the saved and the unsaved—and we would expect that one as holy as Margaret would practice what she preaches. Yet we are struck by a merciless, hypocritical piety which becomes apparent when Luke returns home and collapses. In spite of her husband's need, Margaret refuses to postpone her trip to Philadelphia because "the Lord made me leave that man in there a long time ago because he was a sinner. And the Lord ain't told me to stop my work . . ." (31). Here we have the curious paradox of the woman of God who refuses to help an unsaved brother—her husband—precisely because he is a "sinner." Margaret has other souls to save.

When we consider the allusions to fancy cars and good times which the Philadelphia congregation seems to enjoy, the ostensible purpose for her visit lies open to question. This is particularly true in light of the apparent neglect of her own congregation, as seen when Sister Moore raises the question of Margaret's visit to Sister Rice's mother while Sister Boxer listens. The two women begin to empathize with Margaret because the Philadelphia visits have left her with her "hands full," but Sister Boxer recognizes the hypocrisy inherent in their pastor's priorities and counters, "She got her hands full right down there in her own house. Reckon she couldn't get over to pray for your mother, Sister Rice, she couldn't stay here to pray for her own husband" (47).

### III  "A Fatal Weakness"

The social significance of the play, as I have suggested, is paramount. On this level the familiar Baldwin theme of the search for identity becomes apparent. Fred L. Standley's succinct analysis of the significance of this quest in Baldwin's writings provides a context for my consideration here:

This search or quest for identity is indispensable in Baldwin's opinion, and the failure to experience such is indicative of a fatal weakness in human life. . . .

The quest for identity always involves a man with other men—there can be no self-perception apart from or outside the context of interpersonal relationships. Only within the dynamic interplay of personalities can men become profoundly aware of the significance of being a man. Baldwin sees the lack of interpersonal relations as explicitly related to the breakdown of communication between persons—specifically 'the breakdown of communication between the sexes'. . . .[3]

Luke appears in Act I, and we soon discover that David believes his father had abandoned him. But it is Margaret who is guilty of desertion. She had interpreted the death of their second baby as a sign from the Lord to leave her husband and find a "hiding place." She finds sanctuary in the church because all other doors are closed to her, and she begins her quest for self as a minister of God. But, as Standley's comments indicate, Margaret has made a tragic mistake which is revealed when Mrs. Jackson comes forward to have Margaret pray for her ailing baby:

> MARGARET: Maybe the Lord wants you to leave that man.
> MRS. JACKSON: No! He don't want that! (14)

Mrs. Jackson refuses Margaret's advice because she has already discovered that her identity can only be achieved through an open line of communication with her husband. Margaret has yet to realize this.

The parallel story of the two women becomes even more significant when we consider the sharp contrast which Baldwin makes. In Act III, after her baby has died, Mrs. Jackson tells Margaret, "I ain't like you, Sister Margaret. I don't want all this, all these people looking to me. I'm just a young woman, I just want my man and my home and my children" (66). Margaret, too, had lost a child when she was a young woman but instead of standing by Luke, she nagged him to drink because she felt that he was responsible for the baby's death. She deprived Luke and David of the family relationship which each needed so badly, though no more than she herself required. And as Mrs. Jackson stands alone in the church—a young woman who has just lost her second child—she is bewildered and perplexed. Margaret, however, begins to see her own mistake from the past. Realizing that she has taken the wrong road, Margaret reverses the advice that she had given to Mrs. Jackson prior to the baby's death. "Go on home to your husband," she advises compassionately. "Go on home to your man" (67).

In all probability, Luke is the most sensitive and perceptive character in the play. In one of the most memorable scenes, he describes his suffering, and we are moved to empathy and pity. He tells David that he has failed in his quest for identity—not because of his music—but because he has been denied the most basic human quality—love: "I don't believe no man ever got to . . . [who he is inside] without somebody loved him. Somebody *looked* at him, looked *way* down there and showed him to himself—and then started pulling, a-pulling of him up—so he could live" (44).

Luke realizes that Margaret's distorted sense of reality has preclud-
ed the extension of her love and understanding, thereby denying
David the pursuit of his manhood. He knows that any efforts either
to prescribe the terms of that quest or to protect him from its consequences can only result in the pain and misery of failure which he
himself knows only too well. Luke has learned that a man must
strike out, against the odds, if necessary, to discover the meaning of
his own life. And he encourages David to take the first step toward
reaching that goal.

Baldwin skillfully uses the contrasting qualities of vision and
blindness to symbolize Margaret's lack of inner sight as compared to
that possessed by Luke. This juxtaposition becomes particularly
significant near the end of the drama, as the two parents discuss the
boy—Margaret as if he were dead, Luke affirming that he is alive:

> MARGARET: He's gone.
> LUKE: He's gone into the world. He's gone into the world!
> MARGARET: Luke, you won't never see your son no more.
> LUKE: But I seen him one last time. He's in the world, he's living.
> MARGARET: He's gone. Away from you and away from me.
> LUKE: He's living. He's living. Is you got to see your God to know he's
>    living? (86)

The references to "dark" and "white" further serve to draw our
attention to the contrasting moods and heighten our awareness of
these two different reactions to the boy's departure:

> MARGARET: Everything—is dark this morning.
> LUKE: You all in white . . . (86).

Luke's subsequent death occasions Margaret's remorse and
enhances the cognizance of her own identity. She is forced into a
reexamination of those values that have precipitated her misfortune,
and she emerges in the final scene with a fuller understanding of
the error of her ways: "Her triumph . . . is that . . . although she
has lost everything, [she] also gains the keys to the kingdom. The
kingdom is love, and love is selfless, although only the self can lead
one there. She gains herself" (xvi).

## IV   *The Plague of Color*

The dilemma that Margaret encounters in *Amen* reflects the
quandary that Meridian Henry faces in *Blues for Mister Charlie*.[4]

Margaret has sought the means of acknowledging the manhood of
her husband and her son without exposing them to the consequences attendant to the assertion of that manhood in a white-
oriented society. Meridian has decided that "manhood is a
dangerous pursuit here," and he has sought to insulate himself
against the consequences of that quest and to protect his son
Richard from the hazards which have been built into the framework
of society and specifically designed to thwart blacks in the achievement of that goal. Luke and Meridian have accommodated
themselves to this denial. But neither David nor Richard can afford
the luxury of that safety; they are aware that they must venture out,
examine their lives, and forge their own identities.

Luke and Richard serve as catalytic agents that penetrate the
shell of illusion and lead Margaret and Meridian into an awareness
of reality. After Luke's death, Margaret realizes, at last, that she has
been responsible for his predicament as well as for David's dilemma. In the same manner, Meridian Henry's thoughts become introspective after Richard's tragedy, as we shall see in the final scene
of the play.

Far too many critics, in analyzing a work by a black writer, follow
one of three courses of action: They apply the standards of white
society; they lavish multitudes of patronizing epithets and
generalizations; or they scrutinize it for conflicts in black-white
relations, summarily dismiss it as "race literature," and declare it
unworthy of their consideration on the artistic level.

Much of the criticism of *Blues*, I think, has fallen into the latter
category. The inaccurate description, "based on the race issue," is
all too often indiscriminately applied with the attendant implication
that this is the deepest concern of the play. The primary assumption
by such critics seems to be that Baldwin has failed in the transmutation of experience, in the conversion of rage into a recognizable
human emotion. This provides them with the rationale for rejecting
the play, and it camouflages their inability or unwillingness to
assume the pertinent task of dealing with it as an artistic creation.

Louis Phillips, on the other hand, provides one of the few
glimpses of insight into the play. He begins by recounting that on
the surface the drama is concerned with "racial inequality and injustice" and "the shooting of Emmett Till." But he proceeds a step
further in an effort to uncover the deeper concerns and to recognize
"Baldwin's ability to see the white community of a small southern
town through its own eyes and his ability to portray the wider issues

involved in a racial murder: the terrible self-deception that racial murderers must live by."⁵ These "wider issues" motivate Baldwin to delve into the perverted mind of the racist who is obsessed and driven by the sadistic desire to punish, to persecute, and to kill. His tragic fate, Baldwin observes, is precipitated by the evils of a depraved society: "He does not know what drives him to use the club, to menace with the gun and to use the cattle prod. Something awful must have happened to a human being to be able to put a cattle prod against a woman's breasts. What happens to the woman is ghastly. What happens to the man who does it is much worse. Their moral lives have been destroyed by the plague called color."⁶

Thus, we have a play set in Plaguetown, U.S.A., and we have set before us characters whose vision has become so distorted that reality and illusion converge into self-imposed delusions. Existence itself becomes a welter of ambiguities. In light of these equivocations, we must focus our attention on the key issues involved in the play: What is the plague? Who are its victims? How have these victims been affected? What is the source of the plague? Who is responsible for this condition? These questions suggest the scope of our consideration of *Blues* and form the basis of our investigation into the justification for its claim to universality.

We need not speculate about the nature of the plague because Baldwin clearly defines his use of the term in the introduction to the play: "The plague is race, the plague is our concept of Christianity: and this raging plague has the power to destroy every human relationship" (7). Baldwin argues that our society thrives on the inhumanities and indecencies that have been heaped upon its black citizens. It offers a false concept of religion as an escape from the injustices of a white-oriented, white-controlled society on the one hand and as a rationalization for these humiliations on the other. It leads the social order—blacks and whites alike—along the road to perdition, destruction, and chaos.

## A. *Violence, Revenge of the Powerless*

Let us consider the plague of race and its most afflicted victims, Richard Henry and Lyle Britten. Like Bigger Thomas, Richard's mind has been warped by the degradation to which he has been subjected by the white power structure. The corrosive fires of hate burn brightly within him, and he is obsessed, as Phillips points out, with the idea of revenge. This preoccupation, however, has its roots firmly planted in the dominant motif of power. Richard feels certain that his mother has been murdered by whites, and he experiences a sense of frustration because the perpetrators of the crime have gone unpunished. He secretly wishes that on the day of her death his father had been able to stand up in a courageous assertion of his manhood, but instead, he remembers a foot-shuffling, helpless Uncle Tom: "He couldn't say nothing, he couldn't *do* nothing. I'll never forget the way he looked—whipped, whipped, whipped!" (35)

Meridian Henry becomes a living example of the traditional ineffectuality of the black man within the white power structure. Realizing this, Richard has lost hope for correcting this legal imbalance within the system. He comes to envision revenge, then, as the only recourse for redress: "I just wish, that day that Mama died, he'd took a pistol and gone through that white man's hotel and shot every son of a bitch in the place. That's right. I wish he'd shot them dead" (34 - 35). Frustrated by the miscarriage of social justice, he can only counsel the power of violence.

As Richard nourishes the valid but unproven suspicion regarding his mother's death, he begins the construction of a solid, impenetrable wall of bitterness. He cannot single out his mother's murderers for a confrontation, and so he begins to transfer his hostility to whites in general, who are responsible for "all the crimes" and "all the misery" he has ever known. But the root of these atrocities, he reasons, stems from the helpless condition of black people: "It's because my Daddy's got no power that my Mama's dead. And he ain't got no power because he's *black*. And the only way the black man's going to *get* any power is to drive all the white men into the sea" (35). Mother Henry counsels her grandson that hatred is a poison which will ultimately destroy him, but the vivid memory of his mother's needless death, his father's powerlessness, and his own disillusionment have already been transformed into vials of hatred:

I'm going to learn how to drink it—a little every day in the morning, and then a booster shot late at night. I'm going to keep it right here, at the very top of my mind. I'm going to remember Mama, and Daddy's face that day, and Aunt Edna and all her sad little deals and all those boys and girls in Harlem and all them pimps and whores and gangsters and all them cops. And I'm going to remember all the dope that's flowed through my veins. I'm going to remember everything—the jails I been in and the cops that beat me and how long a time I spent screaming and stinking in my own dirt, trying to break my habit. I'm going to remember all that, and I'll get well. (36)

## B. *Beyond Reality: The Sex Mystique*

In sharp contrast to Richard who displays an overt hostility toward whites, Lyle Britten is completely unaware of his prejudice toward blacks. He has lived beyond reality so long that he cannot focus on his own racial attitudes with any degree of objectivity. Accordingly, when Parnell James, the newspaper editor, suggests that he might be responsible for Richard's murder, he retorts, "You sound like I got something against colored folks but I don't. I never have, not in all my life" (27). The tragedy here is one of moral blindness. Lyle has become a perpetrator of crime and misery among black humanity without even a faint awareness of his complicity in these deeds.

When Parnell confronts Lyle about Richard's murder, he argues, "I ain't no murderer. You know that" (25). The implication here is that only white men are murdered; black men are merely put in their places. Parnell accepts this denial. Though unaware of the identity of Richard's murderer, Parnell is fully conscious, nevertheless, of Lyle's previous sexual involvement with Willa Mae, a black woman, and of his subsequent murder of her suspicious husband. Not only does Parnell believe Lyle innocent of murder, but Lyle himself is unable to acknowledge his own guilt—even to himself. Baldwin provides a clear insight into this phenomenon in his introductory notes. He explains that this self-delusion is psychologically necessary for survival: "What is ghastly and really almost hopeless in our racial situation now is that the crimes we have committed are so great and so unspeakable that the acceptance of this knowledge would lead, literally, to madness. The human being, then, in order to protect himself, closes his eyes, compulsively repeats his crimes, and enters a spiritual darkness which no one can describe" (6).

The theme of sexual exploitation is another aspect of the plague of race which Baldwin explores through the consciousness of Lyle Britten, whose attitude toward women of his own race is typical of white males in general. As self-appointed "protectors" of lily-white virtue, they lend support to a remark made by the state prosecutor during Lyle Britten's trial: "A white woman who surrenders to a colored man is beneath all human consideration. She has wantonly

defiled the temple of the Holy Ghost" (148). This is the white myth
to which Lyle has subscribed because he is sexually insecure. Thus
he employs it as an unwritten condemnation of all who transgress
Divine Law and violate the "purity" of the race.

A second myth that Lyle accepts with equal authenticity is that of
black male sexual superiority. Hence, he is firmly convinced that
"mixing" will lead to interracial sex and ultimately, he fears, to the
invasion of his own bed. In the middle of Act I, he declares to
Parnell, "I'll be damned if I'll mix with them. That's *all*. I don't
want no big buck nigger lying up next to Josephine and that's
where all this will lead to and you know it as well as I do! I'm
against it and I'll do anything I have to stop it, yes I will" (27).
There is, however, a dichotomy here. For Lyle, "mixing" is a one-
way street which leads to the "defilement" of white women by
black men. Nevertheless, he is driven by an insatiable lust for black
women, and he feels free to boast that he can "vouch for the fact"
that not many black virgins are left in the town. In Richard's words,
Lyle is symbolic of the white man who is free to "rape and kill our
women and we can't do nothing. But if we touch one of their dried
up, pale-assed women, we get our nuts cut off" (41).

Richard, like Lyle, has also accepted the black male sex mystique.
Having been denied the opportunity to influence the swing of the
social pendulum, he takes pride in the only realm of authority in
which he feels himself capable: sexual power. He boasts to Pete
about his sexual exploits with white women in Greenwich Village as
a means of increasing his own self-esteem: ". . . they can't get
enough of what little Richard's got—and I give it to them, too,
baby, believe me. You say black people ain't got no dignity? Man,
you ought to watch a white woman when she wants you to give her
a little bit. They will do anything, baby, *any*thing! . . ." (41) Pete
is somewhat amazed that he has taken money from these women,
and as the conversation continues, Richard's attitude toward his
own sexuality (and that of the white male as well) becomes even
more apparent: "Every one of them's got some piss-assed, fagoty
white boy on a string somewhere. They go home and marry him,
dig, when they can't make it with me no more—but when they
want some loving, funky, down-home, bring-it-on-here-and-put-it-
on-the-table-style—" (42). Juanita interrupts, "They sound very sad
. . ." and Baldwin continues to probe deeper into the recesses of
Richard's mind. We become aware that these adventures are

motivated not by lust or revenge, but by the sheer satisfaction of power: "Well, I want *them* to be sad, baby, I want to screw up *their* minds forever . . ." (42).

For Richard, then, these women have become symbols of white domination and oppression. By virtue of their color alone, he has identified them as accomplices in a massive conspiracy to which his mother, his father, his aunt, and he himself have fallen victims. In fact, this is his opportunity to retaliate in behalf of every black man on the face of the earth. And he welcomes the chance to strike back!

## C.  *When the Battle Lines are Drawn*

After Lyle has been tried and acquitted, he breaks down and admits his crime to his wife. His rationale is clearly reflective of the warped, twisted psyche from which he suffers: "I had to kill him. I'm a white man! Can't nobody talk that way to me!" (157) Equally contemptible and indicative of this sickness is the totally indifferent response which Josephine makes to his admission of guilt: "Come on, Lyle. We got to get on home. We got to get the little one home. . . . He's hungry. I got to feed him" (157). Unmoved by Lyle's description of the wanton murder, Josephine has preoccupations far beyond those of the violation of black humanity.

For Lyle and Josephine, those actions that cannot be justified in the name of humanity must be rationalized in the light of racial superiority. George identifies with this concept when Parnell reminds him that he did not have to compete with blacks for his job as shoe salesman. He is forced to acknowledge that he has no other qualification for the job other than his race: "Well, goddammit, white men come before niggers! They *got* to!" (77)

Pseudo-liberalism is symbolized in the play by Parnell James, the local newspaperman who tries to stake his claim in the best of all possible worlds: Full membership in the white race and complete acceptance among those in the community who are black. In befriending Meridian and Lyle, Parnell overextends himself, and we discover that he is regarded with suspicion and cynicism by both races. These misgivings eventually give rise to an open confrontation between Parnell and a group of whites in the kitchen of the Britten home. All whites, these people feel, should be united in their efforts to keep the black man in his place. But Parnell is the renegade, the "Communist," who preaches social justice for blacks.

He is "*worse* than a nigger" because he cannot be trusted. As Reverend Phelps joins the conversation, he tells Parnell that the situation "has become much too serious for flippancy and cynicism." The battle lines have been drawn, and he must take a side: "Are you with us or against us? . . . We've put up with your irresponsibility long enough. We won't tolerate it any longer. Do I make myself clear?" (74)

This same wariness is also shared by the blacks in the community. After Richard has been killed, Meridian begins to reexamine his own attitudes and values, and this serves to objectify the growing distrust of white "liberalism." Believing, like Phelps, that blacks are a "simple people," Parnell cannot understand the bitterness that Meridian now feels toward whites. This failure, Meridian concludes, is symbolic of Parnell's own inability to perceive the black man as a human being with human emotions. This lack of sensitivity is discovered by Meridian as Parnell and the Police Chief discuss Richard's murder: "For both of you—I watched this, I never watched it before—it was just a black boy that was dead, and that was a problem. He saw the problem one way, you saw it another way. But it wasn't a *man* that was dead, not my *son*—you held yourselves away from *that!*" (57)

Parnell's real test, however, comes when he is called upon to testify at Lyle Britten's trial. At this crucial point in the drama, Parnell is in a position to help effect the "social justice" to which he gives lip service in his newspaper. He is now able to function as an agent for positive change in the black community. But he cannot contradict Josephine Britten's testimony because she is *white*. Unable to reject the concept of white supremacy and the cultural institutions of power which it symbolizes, he finds himself incapable of serving the ends of justice. Hence, for Baldwin, Parnell becomes typical of all "liberals" who "are operating in this part of the forest because this is where they find themselves, and it is easy for them—but it has nothing whatever to do with love or justice or any of the things they think it has to do with. And when the chips are down, it comes out. Their status in their own eyes is much more important than any real changes."[7] Parnell's inability to rise to this challenge is not his own unique affliction; it is the plague of race which afflicts the entire community. It is the blind adherence to a creed which demands that justice and humanity be defined explicitly in terms of whiteness.

## D. *Darkness and Light*

The two ministers—Reverend Phelps and Reverend Henry—both serve as vehicles for the development of Baldwin's views concerning the second aspect of the plague, our concept of religion: ". . . the principles governing the rites and customs of the churches in which I grew up did not differ from the principles governing the rites and customs of other churches, white. The principles were Blindness, Loneliness, and Terror, the first principle necessarily and actively cultivated in order to deny the two others."[8] We take Reverend Phelps as tangible evidence of this blindness in the white community. When Lyle is arrested, he is among the whites who visit him in order to reassure him of their support: "We only came by to let you know that we're with you and every white person in this town is with you" (77). Thus, Phelps is able, in good conscience, to console his parishioner who has yet to be brought to trial. The God that Phelps represents permits him the luxury of partiality: Innocent or guilty, he is with Lyle because they both are white. This attitude is similar to the perverse reaction that Lorenzo exhibits in his comments on Richard's death: "This damn almighty God . . . don't care what happens to nobody unless, of course, they're white . . ." (15). In order to understand this attitude, we must recognize the fact that both Lorenzo and Phelps have been taught that "This world is white. . . . White people hold the power, which means that they are superior to blacks (intrinsically, that is: God decreed it so), and the world has innumerable ways of making this difference known and felt and feared."[9]

There is nothing mystifying, then, about Phelps' inability to understand black people and to provide a true Christian perspective for the guidance of his parishioners. Phelps' religion is a spirituality of convenience which functions to reinforce the "superior worth" of the white man in our society. The purpose of the local civil rights demonstrations escapes him because he lacks the objectivity with which to view the black man's struggle for equality. Instead, he attributes the black reaction to injustice to outside influences: "They're a simple people—warm hearted and good-natured. But they are easily led, and now they are harkening to the counsel of these degenerate Communist race-mixers. And they don't know what terrible harm they can bring on themselves—and on us all" (70). It is far easier to blame the problems of a society on forces that lie outside of that society than it is to recognize and embrace reality. And this is the road that Phelps has conveniently taken.

Reverend Meridian Henry, obviously enough, stands as the symbol of religion in the black community. Having been deprived of the dignity of manhood in the secular world, he seeks this respectability in the world of religion: "I've had to think—would I have *been* such a Christian if I hadn't been born black?" (56) For him, dignity is defined in the simplest terms which any husband and father might require: the protection of his wife and his son. Why is it, then, that his concept of religion has resulted in the formulation of values that have been just as ineffectual as the religious convictions to which Phelps adheres? First of all, Meridian uses religion as an escape mechanism to protect himself from the stark realities of life. In strictly ostrich-like fashion, he has stuck his head into the sand of religion, using the Bible as a shield and a solution to the multiplicity of real problems in a real world ruled not by the word of God but by the written and unwritten laws of men. He seeks to deal with the secular world strictly in accordance with Biblical precept, and he finds that this course of action is insufficient: His son and his wife have been wantonly killed by the plague of hate.

Slowly, Meridian becomes aware that yesterday's ineffective solutions will not provide answers to the problems of today. Established values must be reexamined and new ones created in order to deal effectively with these issues. He acknowledges his role as a leader of his people: It is to him that generations yet unborn will turn for a sign, and he does not yet know what that sign must be:

Now, when the children come, my Lord, and ask which road to follow, my tongue stammers and my heart fails. . . . But can I ask the children forever to sustain the cruelty inflicted on them by those who have been their masters, and who are now, in very truth, their kinfolk, their brothers and their sisters and their parents? . . . I have set my face against the darkness, I will not let it conquer me, even though it will, I know, one day, destroy this body. But, my Lord, what of the children? What shall I tell the children? (105)

Meridian begins to move toward these new values, and in Act III we see on the witness stand a man whose faith has begun to falter under the oppressive forces exerted by a society that has been blinded by the plague of race: ". . . both my son and I have profound reservations concerning the behavior of Christians. He wondered why they treated black people as they do. And I was unable to give him a satisfactory answer" (134). Thus he has begun to come to grips with himself. He comes to the awareness that being a man in the sight of God is not enough. But he must, in fact, stake his claim to manhood in the world of men. He now feels compelled to stand before the court, a microcosm of the local power structure, and declare, "I am a man. A *man*! I tried to help my son become a man. But manhood is a dangerous pursuit, here. And that pursuit undid him because of *your* guns, *your* hoses, *your* dogs, *your* judges, *your* lawmakers, *your* folly, *your* pride, *your* cruelty, *your* cowardice, *your* money, *your* chain gangs, and *your* churches . . . (136).

Finally Meridian discovers the answer that he must pass on to posterity. In the closing scene outside the courthouse, Mother Henry issues the call for a prayer march. Meridian, however, has learned that prayer is only half the answer which he must give: "You know, for us, it all began with the Bible and the gun. Maybe it will end with the Bible and the gun" (157). We must not ask God to do for us that which we can do for ourselves. He has made us men biologically, but to us falls the responsibility of asserting our manhood within the social context. It is incumbent upon us to employ both the Bible and the gun—to use nonviolence as well as violence in order to achieve this end.

The final question that Baldwin raises in *Blues* is one of account-ability. Each of us, as members of the universal brotherhood of man, Baldwin contends, has a solemn moral obligation to under-stand the white racist and to attempt the liberation of his children because the responsibility for this man's crimes falls squarely upon he shoulders of the American people: ". . . it is we who put the attle-prodder in his hands. . . . It is we who have locked him in the prison of his color. It is we who have persuaded him that Negroes are worthless human beings, and that it is his sacred duty, as a white man, to protect the honor and purity of his tribe. . . . It is we who have made it mandatory—honorable—that white father should deny black son" (7). Our only salvation, then, lies in our children—white and black. It is they who must help us to become "equal to ourselves." Only they can lead us "to become a people so free in ourselves that we will have no need to fear others and have no need to murder others" (135).

### V    *Crisis of Identity: Ignorance to Freedom*

The assertion of manhood emerges again as one of the major issues in *One Day, When I Was Lost.*[10] Meridian Henry, after much agonizing and soul-searching, became convinced that he might obtain dignity *within* the existing social order. In contrast, Malcolm X is equally confident that self-respect can be obtained only through the creation of a new, independent society which is attuned to the needs of the black man. Both Malcolm and Meridian, as characters created by Baldwin, are keenly aware of the problem of achieving dignity for the black man; only the solutions to this problem set these two men apart.

It is not difficult to understand why Baldwin selected Alex Haley's *The Autobiography of Malcolm X* as the basis for his third dramatic effort. In spite of his disdain for the doctrine of hate espoused by the Black Muslims, Baldwin had always maintained a deep and abiding admiration for Malcolm the man. Moreover—and most importantly—Malcolm X, like the characters that abound in Baldwin's fiction, is a man in search of himself. Therefore, the title is of grave significance because it suggests the identity crises that transform a bewildered, self-effacing Malcolm Little into the energetic, confident, and charismatic Minister Malcolm X, and it foreshadows the keen, inquiring mind that ultimately precipitates the ideological break with Elijah Muhammad.

In Baldwin's hands the flashback becomes a masterful technique which traces Malcolm's development from his birth in Omaha, Nebraska, to his assassination on a Harlem platform in 1965. Throughout the scenario, poverty, racism, drug-addiction, and prostitution contrast sharply with the qualities of pride, dignity, and ambition, all of which influenced the life and career of Malcolm Little. Baldwin succinctly presents these experiences as a kaleidoscopic panorama which gradually unfolds before us. The Little house is set afire by whites; the white firemen, joining the crowd of other whites, allow it to burn; the white mob, after bashing in Earl Little's skull, hurl his body into the path of a streetcar; the white insurance company refuses to pay Earl's death benefit; the white welfare worker succeeds in having Louise Little confined to a mental institution; the white teacher advises Malcolm to enter carpentry instead of law as a more "suitable" vocation; and the white judge sentences Malcolm to eight to ten years in prison for petty theft. Basically, these are the experiences that Baldwin transforms into scenes which constantly flash back and forth in Malcolm's memory, impinging past upon present, and we are thus constantly aware of these forces which serve to shape the psychic development of young Malcolm Little into the fiery exponent of

Black Muslim doctrine and pave the way for the emergence of Malcolm X, founder and leader of Muslim Mosque, Incorporated.

The basic structure of the drama involves four psychological movements and their corresponding physical counterparts which together describe Malcolm's progression from complete darkness toward the light of self-knowledge:

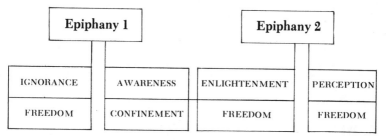

| Epiphany 1 | | Epiphany 2 | |
|---|---|---|---|
| IGNORANCE | AWARENESS | ENLIGHTENMENT | PERCEPTION |
| FREEDOM | CONFINEMENT | FREEDOM | FREEDOM |

The first movement presents Malcolm the pimp, junkie, numbers-runner, bootlegger, and second-story man. A functional illiterate, he enjoys the status of a black stud, complete with "conked" hair, zoot suits, and knob-toe shoes. Finally, Malcolm is arrested, tried, and sentenced to serve a long prison term.

The initial epiphany occurs during Malcolm's incarceration and occurs at the beginning of the second stage of development, awareness-confinement. Through his friend Luther's teachings, Malcolm comes to realize that the Nation of Islam is the true and natural religion for all black men. This moment of insight results in a gradual rejection of the "crutches" of his former life. Giving up his "process," he renounces Christianity and vows to abstain from liquor, cigarettes, and narcotics. On Luther's advice, he begins to study for self-improvement and to embrace the strict code of morality demanded by Muslim affiliation. Thus, we have the paradox of a religious and intellectual freedom born in the midst of physical confinement.

As Malcolm's academic studies progress, he grows in self-confidence. Having been thrust suddenly into the world of books, he becomes a voracious reader, eager and receptive to the knowledge afforded by the printed page. Soon he is able to face an audience, and he joins the debating club which becomes an outlet for the expression of the concurrent religious awareness which he experiences. By the time his release from prison is accomplished, he has undergone a spiritual enlightenment. In this third phase we witness his rapid rise from believer to member, assistant pastor, minister, and organizer in the Nation of Islam under the leadership of Elijah Muhammad.

In the final movement, the second epiphany, which Malcolm experiences in the holy city of Mecca, precipitates his quasi-separation from Black Muslim ideology. Here in the Muslim world, Malcolm witnesses the true fellowship and goodwill of men of all races and color, and his enlightenment is developed and refined into a state of perception. Accordingly, he is compelled to qualify the myth of Yacub which is basic to Muslim belief, and he arrives at a conclusion which directly conflicts with the teachings of Muhammad: Not all whites are blue-eyed devils, unequivocally committed to the psychological and physical destruction of the black man.

The ideological dichotomy which arises as a result of this second epiphany is indicative of another paradox that exists within the Muslim movement itself, as C. Eric Lincoln points out: "As a religion, the Movement is also a paradox. It is a legitimate sect; yet it teaches from the Bible, and it rejects certain of the cardinal Moslem doctrines, notably those of panracial brotherhood and the unique divinity of Allah. The movement is vauntedly anti-Christian, yet it taunts the white man by measuring him against his own high Christian principles—a tactic that implies a strong, though disillusioned Muslim respect for Christian ideals. . . ."[11] For Baldwin, the drama becomes the vehicle through which he illustrates this "respect for Christian ideals." Throughout the drama he juxtaposes Muslim doctrine and numerous allusions to Christianity. Luther tells Malcolm about the white man's efforts to obscure the history of the black man, and he declares, "They don't want black men to hear the truth. That's why any black man even tries to tell the truth is murdered by these white devils . . ." (143). Hence, we are reminded of the Roman throng who chose the thief Barabas over Christ and of the Sanhedrin Council who sentenced Christ to death. Another remark made to Malcolm by Luther suggests Christ, the Savior, sent by God: "I know a black man sent by Allah to rescue this black nation" (144).

The black race is considered "a nation lost in this wilderness for a long time," and Luther relates that "Allah has sent us a prophet who will help us clean up our lives—" (146) as Moses was sent to lead the Israelites out of Egypt. The story of Malcolm's conversion is also strikingly allusive to the story of Christ. Luther informs the prisoners that "I ain't got long to stay here, men, . . ." and he calls

Malcolm aside. His counsel to him suggests Christ's promise to the dying thief: "Me and the leader will both be in touch with you—so don't lose heart. . . . When you come out, you come straight to me" (158 - 159).

After his release from prison, Malcolm hears Lorraine describe Allah and her husband Luther as "not exactly a man like other men" (169); and as a Muslim convert, he reflects upon his experience, "I do not know the man yet, but I know the man who knows the man . . . this man has saved my soul" (165).

There are other ironies as the story unfolds. Earl Little, for example, the one-eyed prophet, half-seeing the superficialities of life, possesses a comprehensive insight into human nature. Malcolm comments that Harvard lawyers, exponents of the "equal justice under the law" philosophy, are trained to keep blacks in jail. And there is the double-irony of Luther, who is intellectually free, yet physically imprisoned, as contrasted with Malcolm before his incarceration, when he was imprisoned in spirit, yet free in body.

By the end of the drama, Malcolm lies mortally wounded. We have seen a thinking man who is able to exchange his past life of debauchery for the strict moral code of the Muslims. And he, the thinking man, is forced to reconcile the Muslim teaching of brotherhood with his own experiences. We have witnessed his progression along the road of self-identity but, like Ralph Ellison's Invisible Man, he does not seem to have arrived at the goal of complete self-realization. Few of Baldwin's characters do. After all, life may be, at best, a series of movements which involve a perpetual "coming along." Perhaps it is the unrelenting, though vital search for an unattainable goal.

A thorough comprehension of the artistry that Baldwin has set before us in these plays requires a transcendence of the peripheral and purely temporal aspects to a consideration of the deeper, interpersonal relationships which exist from generation to generation and from nation to nation. These are the broader issues with which we must contend if ever we are to escape "the terrible darkness" and bear witness to "the reality and the power of light."[12]

## CHAPTER 5

# The Confrontation of Experience

ONE of the most devastating aspects of Baldwin criticism is what seems to be the widespread and almost unanimous assumption among white critics that James Baldwin speaks for the black man. As a corollary to this conclusion, it follows that much of the existing critical opinion has been based on a social perspective, aimed at viewing the essays as a means of justifying Baldwin's role as black "spokesman." In his assessment of the "new luster" that Baldwin brings to the essay as a genre, Irving Howe contends that he is now "one of the two or three greatest essayists this country has ever produced" and that recently he has "emerged as a national figure, the leading spokesman for the Negroes. . . ."[1] David Levin, motivated by a similar persuasion, begins his discussion of the autobiographical essays with the supposition that "Baldwin has come to represent for 'white' Americans the eloquent, indignant prophet of an oppressed people, a voice speaking in print, on television, and from the public platform in an all but desperate, final effort to bring us out of what he calls our innocence before it is (if it is not already) too late."[2] The views of these two critics seem to be typical of the spokesman advocates who fail to consider the significance of the essays beyond their value as sociological treatises.

This critical trend ultimately serves to substitute social for artistic status and to deny the aesthetic achievement of Baldwin's writings. It would be futile to deny the tremendous impact that the essays have had on society, but equally certain is the vigor and authenticity of Baldwin's artistic achievement. Each serves as an indispensable facet of his art.

I  *The Spokesman-Artist Dilemma*

The question of Baldwin the spokesman versus Baldwin the artist has been discussed for more than a decade. At the heart of the matter is the necessity for the separation of "spokesman" from "artist" in order to evaluate more effectively Baldwin's literary contribution. This argument was convincingly advanced by Augusta Strong in 1962: "If we can determine that Baldwin is first of all an artist, no matter how many white audiences solicit his interpretation of Negro problems, and if we will look at him as a writer and not as our self-appointed spokesman, then it becomes more easy to assess what he is and where he succeeds or fails."[3]

The following year, two events seemed to cloud the issue further: the racial crisis which transpired during the spring and summer of 1963 and the appearance of Baldwin's third volume of collected essays, *The Fire Next Time*. The impact of these occurrences, according to Edward Watson, was twofold: It accomplished the widespread reception of the book and simultaneously established Baldwin as "a civil rights pamphleteer . . . [thereby confirming] the identification of the author with things sociological rather than literary. . . ."[4] Watson and Strong both agree on the need for a reevaluation of this aspect of Baldwin's artistry.

Baldwin's own attitude on this subject has been somewhat ambivalent. On June 17, 1962, in a *New York Herald Tribune* book review, he is quoted as saying, "I can't be a spokesman for the American Negro. I speak for some people, but there are others who look upon me as a traitor. . . ."[5] Exactly a year later, in an interview for the same newspaper during the racial conflict, Baldwin denied this role entirely:

The country is going through a crisis and I've been thrown up as this kind of public figure because I'm the top Negro in the country—whatever that means. . . . It's like Sidney Poitier being America's only Negro movie star. That's the country's fault, not ours. But I'm still trying to speak just for me, not for twenty million people. . . . You know, the real point is that people like me and Harry Belafonte and even Martin Luther King are not Negro *leaders*. We're doing our best to find out where the people are and to follow them.[6]

Apparently this difficulty in assessing Baldwin's works is primarily of an external nature in the sense that the gravity of the problem seems to diminish from the author's perspective. In a later statement on a related matter, Baldwin indicates that he has accepted and reconciled the spokesman-artist dilemma: "The dichotomy of my being a spokesman for civil rights and my being a novelist is not as great as it might appear. . . . There's no essential conflict, except in terms of time, and the mechanics that surround speaking in public, and the results of it, which are misleading in another way, because they give you a kind of aura which is not exactly yours. . . ."[7] It is precisely this "aura" which retards literary assessment of the essays and gives rise to a great deal of the existing social criticism. Hence, the task at hand is to consider Baldwin's achievement in the collected essays from the perspective of style and technique in order to justify their existence as artistic creations, to discuss the dominant themes and their sociological significance, and to analyze the rap sessions involving Baldwin, Margaret Mead, and Nikki Giovanni from a sociological viewpoint.

## II  *The Essay As Art: Style and Technique*

The substitution of social for artistic criticism seems to be based upon the underlying assumption that the power of fact is the motivating force in the essays. If this were true, these writings would be reduced to the propaganda of a sociological treatise, and as such, they would be robbed of the tremendous reader appeal that they have elicited. Howard Levant, in an unusually perceptive discussion of the essays, contends that "artistic power, not the facts alone, shocks the Caucasian 'out of his skin' by forcing him to enter the artistic construct, the feeling of being a Negro in America, both in the reading and in remembering the reading. . . ."[8] And in so doing, Baldwin is, in effect, compelling not only whites, but blacks as well, to abandon their cherished illusions and enter into a confrontation with the American experience. This is the technique that he employs in order to "free himself altogether as artist from the distortion of propaganda—the threat of either self-pity or violence—to which all writers are prone by the nature of their work. He has managed thereby to control materials, to imprint form on vagueness, and, in the resulting paradox of art, the rationally, perhaps coldly fashioned prose is tremendously, almost unbearably moving. . . ."[9] It will be profitable, then, to analyze the artistic power of Baldwin's language as the key to his style and technique.

Perhaps the "unbearably moving" quality of the prose in Baldwin's essays grows out of the organic interrelationship of idea and expression, giving rise to an inescapable artistic unity. Consider, for example, the use of repetition as he displays a consummate mastery of rhetoric in recapturing the essence and the spirit of the black man who must "go downtown to meet 'the man' ": "They work in the white man's world all day and come home in the evening to this fetid block. They struggle to instill in their children some private sense of honor or dignity which will help the child to survive. . . . They patiently browbeat the landlord into fixing the heat, the plaster, the plumbing; this demands prodigious patience; nor is patience usually enough. . . ."[10] These tight, parallel constructions, highlighted by the striking subject-verb introductions, convey the sense of frustration and fatigue through the use of a slow, almost monotonous rhythm. The economy of language is also significant here: In three short sentences, Baldwin not only describes the physical condition of the black environment, but he displays remarkable insight into the moral and psychological situation—the perseverance of the elders in their suffering and their dogged determination for the endurance of posterity.

The same techniques are used to create a contrasting effect when Baldwin describes another condition—that of justice for American minorities. With equal economy, he launches a complete denunciation of the legal system in this country, and the reader is drawn into the mood of a raging desperation born of futility and despair: "Ask any Mexican, any Puerto Rican, any black man, any poor person—ask the wretched how they fare in the halls of justice, and then you will know, not whether or not the country is just, but whether or not it has any love for justice, or any concept of it. It is certain, in any case, that ignorance, allied with power, is the most ferocious enemy justice can have."[11] The tone and pace of the passage, the effective use of the repetitive phrase, and the strategic employment of negation clearly reflect the fiery rhetoric of Baldwin the preacher-turned-artist as he attempts to force the reader into a confrontation with reality.

Another aspect of Baldwin's literary talent which scarcely escapes our attention is his use of the catalog. In his hands this device becomes a powerful camera lens which at once focuses on the intolerable conditions that minorities are required to survive in this country every day, on the agents of society who respond zealously to the enforcement of those conditions, and on the terrible blight which this travesty of justice forces upon its victims.

The catalog of situation, which abounds in the essays, is an interesting facet of Baldwin's artistry, as indicated in the passage from *Nobody* which follows: "The wide windows [of the projects] look out on . . . invincible and indescribable squalor: the . . . railroad tracks . . . the unrehabilitated houses, bowed down, it would seem, under the great weight of frustration and bitterness they contain;

the dark, the ominous schoolhouses from which the child may emerge maimed, blinded, hooked, or enraged for life; and the churches, churches, block upon block of churches, niched in the walls like cannon in the walls of a fortress . . ." (60). The explicitness of the simile here is arresting. The church becomes a cannon, a weapon in the wall that blacks have built and maintained for their psychological defense against the abuses of society. This description should be considered also in conjunction with a second, equally vivid ghetto scene which the writer calls to mind in *No Name*: "One walks the long street and sees . . . the shabby pool halls, the shabby bars, the boarded-up doors and windows, the plethora of churches and lodges and liquor stores, the shining automobiles, the wine bottles in the gutter, the garbage-strewn alleys, and the young people, boys and girls, in the streets. Over it all hangs a miasma of fury and frustration, a perceptible darkening, as of storm clouds, of rage and despair . . ." (127). It is not significant that the respective scenes depict Harlem and Watts; they could apply to any black ghetto. What is most striking here is the added dimension of suffering which is conveyed to the reader through Baldwin's keen eye for detail. Thus, what might have been a flat, casual description of two ghetto scenes becomes a delicate blending of physical and psychological details. We see the landscape clearly, but we also *feel* the fury, the frustration, the rage, and the despair.

In another extremely revealing catalog, Baldwin depicts in one Jamesian sentence, the environment, the victims, and their misery which is reflected

in every wine-stained and urine-splashed hallway, in every clanging ambulance bell, in every scar on the faces of the pimps and their whores, in every helpless newborn baby being brought into this danger, in every knife and pistol fight on the Avenue, and in every disastrous bulletin: a cousin, mother of six, suddenly gone mad, the children parcelled out here and there; an indestructible aunt rewarded for years of hard labor by a slow, agonizing death in a terrible small room; someone's bright son blown into eternity by his own hand; another turned robber and carried off to jail. . . .[12]

The mother, the children, and the aunt, ironically enough, are the lucky ones. But what of the robber in jail? What of the blacks and Puerto Ricans in need of a miracle, who have been "trapped in the net called justice?" There is no miracle because there has been a complete abdication of conscience and moral responsibility by the power structure. Baldwin advances this point in *No Name* as he delivers a bitter, satirical denunciation of the American legal system: "The prison is overcrowded, the calendars full, the judges busy, the lawyers ambitious, and the cops zealous. What does it matter if someone gets trapped here for a year or two, gets ruined here, goes mad here, commits murder or suicide here? It's too bad, but that's the way the cookie crumbles sometimes" (148).

In Baldwin's hands, this technique becomes a vehicle that is aimed at overwhelming the reader. And indeed it does just that. The listing of these indignities, these conditions to which white society has become totally apathetic, produces an effect of shocking totality, designed to offset the complacency of illusion.

And the supreme and underlying irony against which these situations must be viewed is that Crispus Attucks and thousands of his nameless black brothers fought valiantly for the liberation *of America,* and their descendants, centuries later—to this very day—continue the fight for freedom *in America.*

Even the most superficial examination of Baldwin's prose style reveals an immense control which he is able to maintain with brilliant success. Evidence of this achievement can be found throughout the essays, particularly in terms of the structural framework upon which Baldwin carefully and succinctly builds his arguments. In "Princes and Powers" (*Nobody*), one of the most notable examples, the author reflects upon the interrelationship of black men in Africa and in America, and he concludes that

there *was* something which all black men held in common, something which cut across opposing points of view, and placed in the same context their widely dissimilar experience. What they held in common was their precarious, their unutterably painful relation to the white world. What they held in common was the necessity to remake the world in their own image, to impose this image on the world, and no longer be controlled by the vision of the world, and of themselves, held by other people. What, in sum, black men held in common was their ache to come into the world as men. And this ache united people who might otherwise have been divided as to what a man should be. (35)

Here we have an antithetical, balanced structure consisting of an introductory statement, two sentences in which Baldwin advances his argument, and two closing statements which function as summation. The eloquence of the argument is further enhanced by the simplicity of the language—the absence of polysyllabic terminology and complex sentence structure—which heightens the clarity and the explicitness of the message.

Another example of Baldwin's ability to frame a cogent argument in lucid terms can be found in "Fifth Avenue, Uptown" (*Nobody*). Here Baldwin effectively gainsays the famous look-how-many-whites-are-in-your-boat-buddy rationale (a variation of the look-how-many-blacks-in-other-countries-are-worse-off-than-you theme and the name-the-handful-of-"important"-blacks-who-prove-you-can-make-it strategy) which is frequently advanced by apathetic whites in answer to black demands for equality:

> Now I am perfectly aware that there are other slums in which white men are fighting for their lives, and mainly losing. I know that blood is also flowing through those streets and that the human damage there is incalculable. People are continually pointing out to me the wretchedness of white people in order to console me for the wretchedness of blacks. But an itemized account of the American failure does not console me and it should not console anyone else. That hundreds of thousands of white people are living, in effect, no better than the "niggers" is not a fact to be regarded with complacency. The social and moral bankruptcy suggested by this fact is the bitterest, most terrifying kind. (58)

Here we have a precise, balanced reasoning in which Baldwin presents the argument for the opposition in three brief sentences. And he moves swiftly and with equal economy in the next three statements to engineer the demolition of the rationale that supports the logic of that argument.

Certainly a brief and initial examination of the aesthetic basis of the essays such as this cannot be regarded as exhaustive. It is, nevertheless, an evaluation that few critics thus far have undertaken. And if it proves true, in the final analysis, that the essays do constitute Baldwin's major contribution to American letters, then it would seem that such an effort in this direction would be an invaluable addition to the body of existing Baldwin criticism.

### III    *The Essay As Art: Theme*

The range and scope of the collected essays span a variety of subjects, all of which serve to illuminate the condition of the black man in twentieth-century America. Richard Rupp has ventured to isolate the major subject of each essay in *Notes*, *Nobody*, and *Fire*, and he has evolved five major categories which have proved useful in this investigation: (1) The Search for Identity; (2) Alienation; (3) The Search for a Usable Past; (4) The Negro as American; and (5) The Need for Love.[13] My analysis of *No Name* and the latest volume, *The Devil Finds Work*, has been in accordance with this method. Based on Rupp's broad categories, the following groupings seem logical points of departure in the discussion of Baldwin's thematic development: (1) The Search for Identity; (2) Alienation; (3) The Black Man as American. The classification of the essays within Rupp's system is selective and, in many instances, at variance with this plan. My objective is to present a representative cross-section of the writings.

## A.   *The Fire Within*

One is scarcely able to avoid the fact that the search for identity is one of the primary forces behind all of Baldwin's writings. For this reason, it has become the theme upon which a majority of the critical attention has been focused. For Baldwin, the key to self-discovery is suffering. He contends in *The Fire Next Time*, for example, that the black man must find a way, however painful, to confront his past "of rope, fire, torture, castration, infanticide, rape; death and humiliation; fear by day and night, fear as deep as the marrow of the bone; doubt that he was worthy of life, since everyone around him denied it; sorrow for his women, for his kinfolk, for his children, who needed his protection, and whom he could not protect; rage, hatred, and murder, hatred for white men so deep that it often turned against him and his own, and made all love, all trust, all joy impossible . . ." (132). He must be able to assess the experiences resulting from this "endless struggle" in order to "achieve and reveal and confirm a human identity . . ." (132). Although many of Baldwin's essays touch upon this subject, his most explicit and comprehensive statements in this regard are contained in "Notes of a Native Son" and "Autobiographical Notes" (*Notes*).

One of the most vivid and graphic aspects of "Notes of a Native Son"[14] is the subtle structure of the essay which gracefully and effectively bears the weight of the theme. Here Baldwin juxtaposes the external violence of the race riots, the attempted assault on a restaurant waitress, and the indignant mob bent on retaliation, to the welter of bitterness raging within, driving the elder Baldwin to insanity and death and jeopardizing the safety of the writer himself:

"I saw . . . that my life, my *real* life, was in danger, and not from anything other people might do but from the hatred I carried in my own heart" (81). His is a hostility, sprung full grown from the pressures of survival, from the oppressive, unbearable "weight of white people in the world" (74). The physical division of the essay itself is also significant. Parts one and two describe the objects of Baldwin's hatred, and part three presents a moving and detailed account of his efforts to come to grips with that inner hostility.

In the initial section, Baldwin recounts his job experiences in New Jersey and the racial prejudice which he encountered there: The rejections at the lunch counter near Princeton, in bars, bowling alleys, restaurants, and rooming houses, all contributed to a "dread, chronic disease" and the obsession " . . . to do something to crush these white faces, which were crushing me" (79 - 80).

Ironically, Baldwin's hostility and bitterness are directed toward blacks as well. And even more revealing is the fact that the second part of the essay focuses upon the elder Baldwin as a victim of the writer's hatred. In his final, delayed visit with his dying father, Baldwin recalls that "I *had* hated him and I wanted to hold on to this hatred. I did not want to look on him as a ruin: it was not a ruin that I hated." (85) He despises his father because the older man is powerless; he has waged a lifelong, bitter, futile struggle against the Establishment to feed nine children. And, finally, he has been defeated by the odds which favor insanity and death over survival.

In part three Baldwin experiences an epiphany. His cognizance of David Baldwin on the funeral bier is accompanied by an equal awareness of his mother and her newborn infant a few blocks away. We have, as Baldwin tells us, death, hatred, and wrong on the one hand, and life, love, and right on the other. And these alternatives become symbolic of the two roads that lie open to the young man: amputation of the gangrenous hatred which "never failed to destroy the man who hated" or liberation of the heart from the corruption and agony of bitterness. The moment of insight is finally reached as Baldwin decides on the latter course. He begins to realize that while life and men must be accepted for what they are, "one must never, in one's own life, accept these injustices as commonplace but must fight them with all one's strength. This fight begins, however, in the heart and it now had been laid to my charge to keep my own heart free of hatred and despair" (95).

This is the awareness to which Baldwin refers in a later essay, "Autobiographical Notes," as he probes into the influences on his writings: " . . . the most difficult (and most rewarding) thing in my life has been the fact that I was born a Negro and was forced, therefore, to effect some kind of truce with this reality . . ." (3). This "truce," the crucial step toward self-identity, has forced Baldwin into an open confrontation with his experience, enabling him to make an honest assessment of his past. Baldwin the man has now been released from his "self-destroying limbo" of hatred, and he experiences a second epiphany which paves the way for the emergence of Baldwin the artist: he begins to understand that "the things which hurt him and the things which helped him cannot be divorced from each other; he could be helped in a certain way only because he could be hurt in a certain way . . ." (2).

Because writing grows from one's experiences, one must not only confront and assess these experiences, but one must *use* them, the "sweet" and the "bitter," in discovering one's own "moral center." Baldwin the artist has been liberated because he has found a way to use his past and to transform those experiences resulting therefrom into art.

## B. *Separate and Unequal*

The theme of alienation is perhaps most effectively pursued in two essays in which Baldwin investigates the estrangement of blacks and whites and Frenchmen and Algerians: "East River, Downtown" (*Nobody*) and "Take Me to the Water" (*No Name*).

In "East River, Downtown" (*Nobody*), Baldwin recalls the demonstrations by blacks at the United Nations following the assassination of Patrice Lumumba. The interesting reaction to this occurrence was that black "spokesmen" were zealous in their affirmation that the sentiments expressed were atypical of the black community. Whites, on the other hand, were denouncing the action as "Communist-inspired."

What is tragic here, as Baldwin points out, is that because the white man has never been able to *see* the horrible conditions of the black ghetto, he persists in the mistaken assumption that, given what they perceive to be the contentedness of blacks, only an outside influence could manipulate and incite black people to riot. But the greater tragedy is that black leaders were led into a position of confirming the illusion which the whites had already accepted for reality.

Aware of the disillusionment of blacks with the "American

Dream," a dream which was never intended for black participation, Baldwin begins to question the fact that nationality and allegiance are considered synonymous where the black man is concerned. But no thought has been given to the rights and privileges to which one is entitled by virtue of that nationality and allegiance. Rebellion against these "peculiar attitudes" is entirely justifiable because blacks "have every right to refuse to be found by a set of attitudes as useless now and as obsolete as the pillory" (72).

The challenge that Baldwin issues is for the recognition that the United Nations demonstration reflects world discontent among blacks. He calls upon the country to accept this fact, and to be prepared to come to grips with the problem and set our own house in order.

"Take Me to the Water" *(No Name)*, stands as a panoramic catalog of the theme of alienation, ranging from North to South: Harlem, Charlotte, Little Rock, Atlanta, Birmingham, and Montgomery. An international dimension is added through an exploration of French-Algerian relations. The essay begins on a personal level in Harlem, sweeps us into a discussion of the brutal harassment of Algerians by the Paris police, and concludes with Baldwin's initial encounters with racism in the South.

In the initial stage the essay takes on the air of repetition as Baldwin recalls not only the estrangement from his father which he felt, but the alienation of his stepbrothers and stepsisters as well. Forced into the role of mediator, Emma Baldwin sought to cushion her children against the merciless abuses of her husband who was finally driven insane by the indignities and frustrations inherent in the black experience: "One had only to take a bus ride from the top of the city and ride through it to see how it was darkening and deteriorating, how human bewilderment and hostility rose, how human contact was endangered and dying" (34).

From this point we are swept with the writer into Paris as Baldwin juxtaposes the atmosphere of Harlem decay with the subjugation of minorities, French style. Having no money, Baldwin was forced to live among *"les miserables,"* the Algerians, who suffered police brutality, overcrowded living conditions, and economic deprivation. Baldwin's flight had grown out of a compelling need to discover "a place where I would be treated more humanely than my society had treated me at home, where my risks would be more personal, and my fate less austerely sealed . . ." (40). And Paris had fulfilled that need by ignoring him. He was considered "different," in spite of the fact that he lived among the Algerians and, as such, he was treated with the utmost courtesy by the French government, in much the same way that many poor whites in America have lived for years in "integrated" neighborhoods without having had to suffer the same discrimination which blacks traditionally have had to endure. Each society has its scapegoats: blacks in America and Algerians in France.

Baldwin returns to another favorite theme here: the relationship of one's past to the quest for identity. He begins to realize that the Algerian dilemma was more "coherent" than the black situation in America. The Algerians, in refusing to yield their history to the French, had proudly retained their past and their home, and one day they would return. But the black man in America has no such coherence because he has been forced to abandon his history; consequently, in a cultural sense, he has no prospect of going "home."

Yet, both blacks and Algerians are "victims of the history" of subjugation, and Baldwin begins to identify with them because of the mutuality of their struggles for the control of destiny. Thus came the awareness that he must return to the battlefield in America and pursue his identity: "It was only here, after all, that I would be able to find out what my journey had meant to me, or what it had made of me" (51).

This decision brings the movement of the essay full circle. Baldwin began his probe of alienation from a personal perspective in Harlem, and now he returns to the United States to continue the exploration of alienation in the South. He recalls feeling the restrained hostility shown by three white men in Alabama as they watched the Montgomery Improvement Association car drive up to the airport to pick him up: "If the eyes of those men had the power to pulverize that car, it would have been done. . . . I had never in all my life seen such a concentrated, malevolent poverty of spirit. . . . No one in authority in the town, the state, or the nation, had the force or the courage or the love to . . . redeem the souls of those three desperate men . . ." (78 - 79).

It is this "malevolent poverty of spirit" that Baldwin finds completely overwhelming. The South, he contends, is possessed by a profound lovelessness, dating back to the dehumanizing practice of American slavery which robbed sexual contact of love, allowing white men to exploit the bodies of black women in the breeding of slaves. As a result, this "money-making conspiracy . . . emasculated them of any human responsibility—to their women, to their children, to their wives, or to themselves [so that] . . . they no longer have any way of knowing that any loveless touch is a violation . . ." (62 - 63). Love, then, becomes a powerful force, an ethical criterion, indispensable to the moral fiber of the South and to the nation as a whole.

## C.  *The Myth of the "American Dream": Image Versus Reality*

The peculiar circumstances surrounding the black man as an American are discussed more explicitly in three essays: "My Dungeon Shook" (*Fire*), "Fifth Avenue, Uptown" (*Nobody*), and "Who Saw Him Die? I, Said The Fly" *(Devil)*. These explorations into the social and moral assumptions upon which this country operates are indeed representative of Baldwin's efforts in nonfiction to investigate beyond the superficialities of the "American Dream" rhetoric and discover those foundations and analyze those institutions that constitute the fabric of the American way of life.

"My Dungeon Shook" *(Fire)* takes on a warmth and intimacy, much like that of a father-son chat, through Baldwin's use of the letter as a personal channel for the communication of his thoughts. He addresses his brother's son in an effort to impress upon him the odds for his survival in America—odds deliberately manipulated in order to minimize and virtually preclude the achievement of success: "You were born where you were born and faced the future that you faced because you were black and *for no other reason*. The limits of your ambition were, thus, expected to be set forever. You were born into a society which spelled out with brutal clarity, and in as many ways as possible, that you were a worthless human being. You were not expected to aspire to excellence: you were expected to make peace with mediocrity . . ." (18).

Unlike many of the other essays, the tone is not inflammatory; it is not intended to incite his namesake to anger. The speaker himself is not bitter; his singular purpose seems to be the stimulation of an awareness within the boy that he cannot afford to play his game of life according to the rules that have been laid down by society. The essay is not a direct indictment of the social system. Rather, it has the effect of providing information that will assist in the development of a counter-strategy for survival.

Baldwin presents young James with a succinct three-point battle plan for his consideration. The message is not new, but the forceful, compelling rhetoric tends to awaken a new sense of dedication to the pursuit of these *coups de main*. The most significant aspect of this strategy is the retention of integrity. Baldwin advises his young nephew that he must maintain an innate belief in his own potential for success; he must reject unequivocally the devious artifices perpetuated by whites to destroy his dignity and block his opportunities for achievement.

Secondly, in counteracting these myths, he must become familiar with his own past, and he must rely solely on the wisdom of his own experience. Because one cannot operate in a void, he exhorts young James never to deny his history or his own experience, but to honor that past and use that experience as a guiding influence in his life.

Black people have been able to survive in the white man's world, Baldwin argues, because they were able to love each other. His third point is that there is an urgent need for the preservation of that love as a motivational force, directed toward the acceptance of white people, who are hopelessly "trapped in a history which they do not understand. . . . We, with love, shall force our brothers to see themselves as they are, to cease fleeing from reality, and to begin to change it . . ." (19 - 21). Love becomes an exonerative power which embodies the "turn the other cheek and love thy neighbor" concept, a principle that has fallen into growing disfavor among blacks in general, many of whom, having been driven to the brink of futility, have begun to adopt the code of Hammurabi: an eye for an eye.

"Fifth Avenue, Uptown: A Letter from Harlem" (*Nobody*), as the title suggests, presents the dilemma of the black man in America from a different perspective: the physical Harlem versus the human elements who inhabit and maintain it. The tone here is one of bitterness and despair. The structure of this essay reflects two distinct aspects of the ghetto. On the one hand we have the dilapidated environment and the victims of that environment; on the other stand the ominous efforts toward ghetto "rehabilitation"—the projects and the callous white policemen hired by the white world to contain that ghetto through whatever means are available and necessary.

The essay begins, typically, with a wide panoramic sweep which reveals a "filthy, hostile Fifth Avenue," symbolic not only of Harlem, but of the American ghetto in general where millions of black people live. There are the grocery stores, the laundries, the shoeshine "parlors," and the "soda-pop joints." There are the gimmicks used to complete the process of exploitation already begun by the food, clothing, and shelter con men who regularly exact their exorbitant prices: " 'wider' TV screens, more 'faithful' hi-fi sets, more 'powerful' cars, all of which, of course, are obsolete long before they are paid for . . ." (59). And there are the houses, long since condemned by their decaying foundations, and the people, devoid of all sense of accomplishment and fulfillment, caught up in the unending struggle for survival.

Baldwin achieves a dramatic effect here by highlighting the human element of the ghetto. We are reminded of those whose physical death has been consummated by means of "World War II, the Korean War, a policeman's gun or billy, a gang war, a brawl, madness, an overdose of heroin, or, simply, unnatural exhaustion" (56), and we are plunged into the lives of the less lucky, those who suffer and survive these agonizing deaths. Some of these people retreat into the spirituality of religion; some exchange Christianity for the theology of the Black Muslims. Others find escape in the narcoticizing effects of the television screen or in the neighborhood drug pusher. Still, there are those who, having survived these physical and psychological deaths, are condemned to "get up in the morning and go down town to meet 'the man' " (57). A few of these, the privileged, are able to make their escape to another "more respectable ghetto."

In the second phase of the essay, we encounter the symbols of ghetto improvement and maintenance—the projects and the policemen, equally hated by blacks because they stand as monuments to the attitude with which blacks are regarded by the white world. Baldwin describes the projects as "cheerless as a prison . . . colorless, bleak, high, and revolting," managed through the employment of the most demeaning policies: salary raises must be reported for raises in rent, and the administration exercises its privacy-invading prerogatives to terminate your occupancy at will and to screen and approve all overnight apartment guests.

The policeman relies on the gun, the badge, and the billy club to intimidate, threaten, maim, and kill in an effort to contain the ghetto. Aware of the degrading circumstances attendant to his job, he adopts a posture of callousness and oppressiveness. He is hated, not for who he is, or for the actions for which he is personally responsible, but for his function in the capacity of a brutal, merciless defender of the power structure. Blacks—young and old alike—are well aware that he exists as a "public" servant who serves not as their protector, but rather as an accomplice in enforcing the oppressing conditions imposed upon black people by the white world.

They know that he has been totally unprepared by the segment of society that he represents to understand that "*Negroes want to be treated like men*" (63). Baldwin concludes the essay with a concise, sweeping indictment of American society: Blacks and whites alike, in the North as well as in the South, are all victims of the social, legal, and political corruption which continues to thrive and flourish in this country.

The theme of image versus reality informs one of Baldwin's newest essays, "Who Saw Him Die? I, Said the Fly" *(Devil)*. Here Baldwin injects a unique element into his examination of the black man as American. Through the medium of film, he conducts a rather detailed analysis of the verisimilitude conveyed by several movies selected at random from his personal experiences.

One of the targets of his sharpest criticism is *The Birth of a Nation*. Baldwin objects to the initial image in the film which depicts the arrival of black slaves in America in European garb with facial expressions that suggest a yearning for America, the land of golden opportunity. He reminds the movie moguls (and white America) that Africans came to these shores with neither European clothes nor an attitude of optimistic anticipation: Blacks were dragged to America naked and in chains. In an earlier discussion, "Liberalism and the Negro," Baldwin asserts that blacks were the only unwilling participants in the great American dream. A second objection concerns the prominent role which mulattoes play and the unrestrained lust for whites which they reveal. Baldwin emerges here in a familiar stance as he uses his artistic skill to gainsay the popular myth that blacks have an unusual sexual attraction to whites.

This scrutiny is continued in *In the Heat of the Night* as Baldwin questions the plausibility of the circumstances surrounding Virgil Tibbs' appearance in a small southern town in the early morning hours. In a later episode, when one of the leading citizens slaps Tibbs and he obligingly reciprocates, the sheriff almost responds, "You had that coming, buddy!" This gives us good reason to doubt the likelihood of a southern white sheriff who abides such actions from a black man, especially when badges are won and lost in small southern towns long before the voters reach the ballot boxes. Baldwin also dwells on the implications of money and power in the film: the sheriff is chagrined because Tibbs earns more money than he does, and we have every reason to shudder at Tibbs' fate until the rich widow decides to use her influence to retain him to track down her husband's murderer.

Under these circumstances, the sheriff must tolerate Virgil, but he is never able to accord him the same degree of respect which a white colleague would command. Yet, Virgil seizes upon clue after clue, and he finally cracks the case in a display of professional crime detection which leaves the sheriff baffled and aghast. Again Baldwin returns to a previous theme as he summarizes the history of the sheriff and the townspeople: "The film helplessly conveys—without confronting—the anguish of people trapped in a legend. They cannot live within this legend; neither can they step out of it" (55 - 56).

Baldwin discusses this legend in conjunction with two other films in which Poitier starred—*The Defiant Ones* and *Guess Who's Coming to Dinner*—and he concludes the essay with a first hand, mortifying and degrading experience with the FBI in 1945. He describes the intimidations, the insults, the shakedowns, the curses, the searches—all conducted in the name of justice—and he decides, quite understandably, that "I loved my country, but I could not respect it, could not, upon my soul, be reconciled to my country as it was" (92). His conclusion becomes inevitable: Hollywood producers have become unwitting conspirators in the dissemination of films which reflect and reinforce the distortions of black reality which abound in our society.

## IV    *"Things Are in the Saddle": Responsibility and Commitment*

These general themes of identity, alienation, and the black man as American also reflect some of the overriding concerns of the books which grew out of the two colloquies in which Baldwin participated in 1971. The first of these, a dialogue with Margaret Mead entitled *A Rap on Race*[15] (1971), was taped in Dr. Mead's New York apartment on August 26 and 27. A subsequent conversation with Nikki Giovanni, *A Dialogue* (1973), was taped in London for the television program "Soul!" on November 4. Nothing is resolved in these two volumes, and yet they stand as enlightening explorations into some of the fundamental issues which form the crux of the American dilemma.

*Rap* begins on the common ground of agreement as Baldwin and Mead discuss the issue of integration versus black power. The quest by the black man for integration into the mainstream of American life has been based on accommodation. Aided in this effort by the Supreme Court decision of 1954 and the civil rights legislation of the 1960s, the black man sought to embrace the cultural standards of white society in an effort to prove his affinity with white Americans, and avoid the frustration of racial discrimination. And as a growing number of whites began to accept this assimilationist doctrine, they encouraged these efforts, thereby accomplishing a different kind of denial, as Dr. Mead points out: "We'll deny your hair, we'll deny your skin, we'll deny your eyes, we deny you. We deny you when we accept you; we deny the ways in which you are not exactly like us, by ignoring them" (12). It is the rejection of this melting pot process that leads Baldwin and Mead to the realization that black power, rather than integration, promises a more feasible solution to the problems of segregation. Both discussants agree that "Democracy should not mean the leveling of everyone to the lowest common denominator. It should mean the possibility of everyone being able to raise himself to a certain level of excellence" (136).

Another recurring concern in this dialogue is the question of tactile communication. Margaret Mead makes the observation that "average, middle-class" white Americans seem determined to suppress the urge to exercise the touch as a means of communication. For Dr. Mead this presents a gap in the process of human intercourse: "I feel if I don't touch, . . . I haven't communicated . . . at all. I could sit across the room and make beautiful speeches forever, but one touch makes the difference, just one touch" (46). It is this necessity for human intercourse and contact that forms the basis of Baldwin's attack on the high-rise ghetto projects in several of his essays. The destruction of the tenements becomes synonymous not only with the destruction of the neighborhood, but with the denial of humanity as well: "There was no longer any communication between the people. There was no longer any way for them to adjust to each other. They were all trapped in these ghastly highrise slums and hating it. People wondered why they broke the windows and peed in the halls, but I know why. They were being corralled into hovels like rabbits; they were not being treated like human beings . . ." (133).

The tactile inhibition manifests itself not only as a means of intraracial hindrance to communication, but also as a method used by whites to drive a wedge between blacks and themselves. This failure to exercise the sense of touch, even in a perfunctory manner, becomes merely another of the thousands of ways of rejecting the humanity of the black man. Even the innocent black child who encounters a white merchant in the neighborhood candy store is quick to recognize the practice of placing change on the counter or dropping it into his hand, instead of handing it to him. And it cannot be because his hands are dirty because he has seen the ritual practiced with his father, his mother, and other blacks as well. This and countless other contrivances and manipulations—both subtle and overt—have led Baldwin to the conclusion that "the great emotional or psychological or effective lack of love and touching is the key to the American or even the Western disease" (146).

The two discussants trace this malady back to the passengers on the Mayflower, who were not the affluent, but the incarcerated, the disinherited, and the poverty-stricken, all preoccupied with the search for wealth, fame, and fortune. This quest has become a dangerous obsession, as Ralph Waldo Emerson reminded us in "Ode": "Law for man, and law for thing"; the latter, uncontrolled, ". . . runs wild, / And doth the man unking." Aware of this immutable law, Dr. Mead is optimistic about the evolution of a "collective" society as a means of coping with this crisis: "What I hope is going to happen in the world is a demand similar to the one in this country, the demand for a simpler form of life. . . . Otherwise what is happening is that other countries are copying this style, so the few educated and elite . . . get themselves some Cadillacs and big houses. Then all of the rest of the people are miserable. Also we are bleeding the world of its resources and we can't afford to do that" (149).

These are perhaps the central issues on which Baldwin and Dr. Mead are in general agreement. Yet there is one topic on which consensus does not seem to exist: the question of guilt and responsibility. During the first phase of the discussion (August 26, 8:00 p.m.), Baldwin laments the fact that acceptance of responsibility for one's deeds seems to be a virtue which has become extinct in American life. He cites, as an example, the "preposterous" explanations given for the Kennedy and King assassinations. At this juncture, the focal point of the discussion shifts to the atomic bombing of Hiroshima. Dr. Mead contends that the term "guilt" is limited to those who had knowledge of and control over the bombing. Having had neither, Dr. Mead disclaims all guilt in the matter, although she is willing to accept the responsibility for working to improve the present and to build for the future. The position that Baldwin establishes here seems to coincide with Dr. Mead's viewpoint:

BALDWIN: What I'm trying to get at is the question of responsibility. I didn't drop the bomb, either. And I never lynched anybody. Yet I am responsible not for what has happened but for what can happen.

MEAD: Yes, that's different. I think the responsibility for what can happen . . . is saying I am going to make an effort to have things changed. But to take the responsibility for something that was done by others—

BALDWIN: Well, you can't do that. (59)

The ideological gap does not become apparent until the third segment of the conversation (August 27, 11:00 p.m.) which is devoted almost exclusively to this issue. Baldwin retreats from his former posture and makes the assertion that one's history is written on one's brow. Mead's counter, consistent with her earlier argument, is a refusal to accept the racial guilt attendant to the injustices perpetrated by her ancestors. She rejects unequivocally the Old Testament concept of the parents' sins falling upon the heads of their innocent children. Baldwin, however, fails to yield the position which he had established earlier in *Blues:* We as a nation are individually and collectively responsible for the crimes committed by the white racist because he is a product of the society which blacks and whites alike have created. Mead denounces this position as Russian orthodox, which accepts the premise of guilt by association:

MEAD: I will not accept responsibility for what other people do because I happen to belong to that nation or that race or that religion. I do not believe in guilt by association.

BALDWIN: But, Margaret, I have to accept it because I am a black man in the world and I am not only in America. . . . I have a green passport and I am an American citizen, and the crimes of the Republic, whether or not I am guilty of them, I am responsible for. (225)

The antipodal views here seem beyond reconciliation. Yet these attitudinal differences provide the key to the final opinions expressed by Baldwin and Mead regarding the question of hope. Dr. Mead, in rejecting guilt by association, assumes responsibility only for that over which she has direct control. She retains an abiding faith in the ability of America to change its charted course, and she is appalled, however unjustifiably, because Baldwin does not share that optimism. However untenable Baldwin's argument may be in terms of the assumption of guilt and responsibility, the fact remains that the terror of the deeds of his countrymen which he assumes upon his shoulders leads logically to the death of the hope that the American Dream is capable of reaching fruition. The body of Martin Luther King and the optimism of Baldwin's dream share a mutual grave: ". . . there was a time in my life not so very long ago that I believed, hoped . . . that this country could become what it has always presented as what it wanted to become. But I am sorry, no matter how this may sound: when Martin was murdered for me that hope ended" (244).

Near the end of the dialogue, Baldwin catalogues the injustices that blacks have endured, and Mead solicits his view of how he intends to become an instrument of social change in this country. Baldwin replies, "Blow it up" (250). This attitude tends to underscore Baldwin's ideological posture of the Sixties and early Seventies, to which I have referred in Chapter 1. It is a position which, further, seems consistent with his closing thoughts in *No Name* (1972): "I know what I would do if I had a gun and someone had a gun pointed at my brother, and I would not count ten to do it and there would be no hatred in it, nor any remorse. People who treat other people as less than human must not be surprised when the bread they have cast on the waters come floating back to them, poisoned" (192). Perhaps the basic differences in Mead's optimism and Baldwin's pessimism lie in the disparity between the black and the white experiences. No issues are solved here, but certainly much insight has been offered.

*A Dialogue*[16] represents the simultaneous wedding of two black poets, the linking of pre- and post-World War II generations, and the ideological communion of a black man and a black woman. The conversation gets off to a brisk start as Baldwin and Giovanni become involved in a discussion of the black image. Baldwin credits Nikki's generation with rejecting the standards of the society in which they were born and effecting a positive change in black people's self-image. Both discussants agree that this has been a significant step forward because our capitalistic society has, in every single instance, provided a frame of reference that denigrated the humanity of the black man. There has never been a "corroboration" of a sense of worth and human dignity, and so blacks have had to develop their own standards and values within a totally different frame of reference.

Throughout the discussion, Baldwin consistently represents the historic point of view, while Giovanni is clearly symbolic of present attitudes. This becomes clear as the poets discuss two aspects of the question of black manhood: male brutality and moral responsibility. For Giovanni, the cruelty typically manifested by the black male toward his family represents an appalling, self-perpetuating phenomenon which seems incredible: "I don't understand how a black man can be nothing in the streets and so fearful in his home, how he can be brutalized by some white person somewhere and then come home and treat me or mother the same way that he was being treated . . ." (43). Baldwin seeks to explain the psychological ramifications attendant to this physical abuse of the family by recounting the awesome "price" demanded of the black man for his masculinity: society's adamant refusal to recognize his male role, the resultant denial of the joys and sorrows of being a man, and the economic exploitation of his children. Robbed of his sexuality, stripped of the ability to love his family and to retaliate upon the oppressor, he finds emotional release in the church and in his own home: "I know something about that. I don't know what happens to a woman but I understand what happens to a man. You cannot do anything. They've got you; they've got you by the throat and balls. And of course it comes out directed to the person closest to you" (46). This is the terrible cost, exacted from human flesh, for the dignity which the black man enjoys today.

The issue of moral responsibility to the black family is pursued by the two artists as a problem which yet persists in this generation. Giovanni ponders the inability of the black male to provide the emotional security which is a vital, indispensable factor in the family unit. She illustrates this point by presenting a fictionalized account of "Maybelle," who has been deserted by her lover because he is unable to offer financial security to her and their unborn child. The economic aspect, she argues, becomes subordinated to the need for the exercise of a moral obligation: "The baby's going to sleep *some*place. The baby's going to eat *some*thing. But what Maybelle needs at that moment is a man. . . . Maybelle understands there is no job. But what she needs is a man to come by and say, Hey baby, you look good. And black men refuse to function like that because they say, I want to bring the crib when I come. You're never going to get the crib" (52). Baldwin counters that this attitude is firmly rooted in the white cultural ethic. And within that framework, manhood is defined explicitly in economic terms. Having accepted that ethic, the black male, however futilely, feels the compelling necessity to function on that level. Unable to meet this criterion, he cannot assume the moral obligation toward his family. What is important to him is not that his family needs his presence, or that they are willing to accept him in spite of his unemployment. He has become a victim of a kind of moral stagnation, precipitated by his own self-recriminations and confirmed by the social climate in which he lives.

Acknowledging this situation, Giovanni calls for a re-definition of manhood as a moral commitment. She makes an admirable attempt to force a reassessment of the questions, "What makes a man? . . . Can you be a man wherever you are and whatever the circumstances?" (58) Women must begin to reject the ethic that denies manhood to their men. They must demand that black men reject the idea of becoming "little white men"; they must insist upon the discovery of a "new base" which will allow their men to pursue their manhood on terms that offer some prospect of success.

Giovanni's position here is underscored by Baldwin's assertion that as an artist, "in any case, the one thing you have to do is try to tell the truth . . ." (74). He must acknowledge the reality of his life; he is bound to make the effort to help us reject the illusions of our own. The artist remains eternally aware of men as they grope within the sordid darkness of their lives in an effort to discover themselves and their relationship to each other. For it is he who can dispel the darkness, bring us into a confrontation with the experiences of our past, and lead us toward a moral commitment to the children of the present and to countless generations yet unborn.

## CHAPTER 6

# The Scheme of Things:
# New Worlds and Beyond

EARLY in his career James Baldwin set out to pursue his lot as a writer and to, accept his solemn obligation to reveal the "multiple truths" of society. And he came to view that society as one constantly in need of overhauling, and equally incapable of accomplishing that end without the prophetic vision of the artist. Refusing to allow his talent to become stagnant and petrified in a conventional mold, Baldwin has been vigorous in his efforts to destroy our restricting, illusive, and self-imposed visions of life and to restore the power and the light of reality.

We have viewed his writings against these social imperatives, but two questions yet remain. What is the nature of Baldwin's literary legacy to twentieth-century American literature? What are some of the problems involved in assessing his artistic stature within the scheme of things? This chapter will involve a consideration of these comprehensive aspects of James Baldwin's artistry.

## I  *From the Ivory Tower:*
*Baraka and Cleaver versus Baldwin*

During the past two decades, James Baldwin has garnered the largest audience of readers among black writers in this country. This single fact has aroused the suspicion and disdain in black militant quarters that Baldwin has made a deal with the Establishment, that he has become, in Eldridge Cleaver's words, one of the "Stepin Fetchits" of the age. Sharing this point of view, Amiri Baraka takes Baldwin to task for an unfortunate declaration which he made in "Autobiographical Notes" *(Notes)* in 1955. During his early years in Paris, Baldwin seems to have struggled with the question of the relationship of the artist to the social and political struggles of black

125

people in America. This dilemma, one of primary significance, encompasses *vita contemplativa* and *vita activa* as two dichotomous, irreconcilable options. Baldwin finally reached the conclusion that these struggles are not the "prime concern" of the writer and that an objective aloofness must be maintained so that the literary responsibility might be discharged. Although he was forced to reverse this posture during the crucial civil rights struggles of the 1960s, the concept of "division of responsibility" proved to be his Achilles heel, and Baraka, among other black militant writers, was quick to seize this blunder and exploit it to his advantage. In a 1963 essay, both Peter Abrahams and Baldwin fall victim to Baraka's verbal barrage for their failure to become involved in the racial struggle:

Men like Baldwin and Abrahams want to live free from such "ugly" things as "the racial struggle" because (they imply) they simply cannot stand what it does to men. . . .

Their color is the only obstruction I can see to this state they seek, and I see no reason they should be denied it for so paltry a thing as heavy pigmentation. Somebody turn them! And then perhaps the rest of us can get down to the work at hand. Cutting throats![1]

Hence, it follows that Baraka's assessment of Baldwin's literary contribution is a negative one (See Chapter 1). Predictably also, Cleaver takes a similar view: "There is in James Baldwin's work the most grueling, agonizing, total hatred of the blacks, particularly of himself, and the most shameful, fanatical, fawning, sychophantic love of the whites that one can find in the writings of any black American writer of note in our time. . . ."[2] Aside from Cleaver's charge of homosexuality (See Chapter 3), he castigates Baldwin for his views on Richard Wright, his attitude on the African-European heritage issue, and his depiction of violence and sex. Let us consider these charges briefly.

As a result of Baldwin's criticism of Richard Wright's *Native Son* in "Everybody's Protest Novel," Cleaver accuses Baldwin of envying Wright's masculinity. Jervis Anderson recognizes this attack as self-serving, and he regards it merely as a subterfuge, an attempt to enhance Cleaver's literary stature at Baldwin's expense.[3] Similarly, for Julian Mayfield, Baldwin has attained the stature of a "comfortably well off . . . literary god," the "natural target" for Cleaver's verbal abuse.[4] In his eloquent rebuttal to Cleaver's argument, Addison Gayle astutely observes that Cleaver has failed to attend Baldwin's argument; he has confused Wright the cultural hero with Wright the novelist: "One can understand if not sympathize with Cleaver's desire to avenge the name and honor of Richard Wright. Negroes have had few cultural heroes of the stature and magnitude of Wright. . . . But it is one thing to admire Wright as a cultural hero, and quite another to deal with him as a novelist. . . . In 'Everybody's Protest Novel,' Baldwin's criticism is that of the critic, and he has hit at a fundamental weakness of *Native Son*. . . ."[5]

Another stratagem that Cleaver employs in Wright's defense is the condemnation of Baldwin's art for its depiction of homosexuality and its association of violence with sex. He extols the naturalistic quality of *Native Son*, compares it with several of Baldwin's writings, and concludes that

Richard Wright reigns supreme for his profound political, economic, and social reference. Wright had the ability, like Dreiser, of harnessing the gigantic, overwhelming environmental forces and focusing them, with pinpoint sharpness, on individuals and their acts as they are caught up in the whirlwind of the savage, anarchistic sweep of life, love, death, and hate, pain, hope, and pleasure, and despair across the face of a nation and the world. . . .

And Bigger Thomas, Wright's greatest creation, was a man in violent, though inept rebellion against the stifling, murderous, totalitarian white world. . . .[6]

This assessment of Richard Wright seems fair and accurate, but it does not provide the grounds upon which a differentiation of the work of the two writers can be based because Baldwin's writings also merit the same judgment. Consider, for example, the characters Richard and Meridian Henry in *Blues*. Both father and son find themselves caught in the web of futility. They are powerless creatures who are struggling to assert their manhood in society against overwhelming odds. They are victims of physical violence and sexual exploitation which, wedded, become twin monsters bent on human destruction. Similarly, the short stories in the collection *Going to Meet the Man* further illustrate this fatalistic quality. In "Previous Condition," Peter recalls a childhood in which his parents suffered the endless abuses of the whites who controlled their lives. And as an aspiring young artist, he finds himself subject to the same frustrations. Compelled to fight the white world, he is driven nearly insane in his efforts to cope with the brutal, inhumane facts of life. "This Morning, This Evening, So Soon" sketches the life of a black singer who has escaped a brutally repressive childhood to find fame and fortune in Paris. Unable to forget the rape of one of his sister's friends by two white policemen and his degrading experiences as an elevator boy in a white department store in Alabama, he becomes obsessed with the desire to pursue his admittedly futile efforts to protect his young son from the humiliating experience of being black in America. These writings seem to fit within the range and scope of Cleaver's evaluation of Wright, and, as such, they invalidate the distinction that he makes between the two artists.

Cleaver also attacks Baldwin for his admission in *Notes* that, as an adolescent, he found it necessary to embrace white American cultural values because his African heritage had been completely destroyed. Only self-hate, Cleaver argues, could motivate such a decision. Consequently, in Cleaver's eyes, Baldwin becomes guilty of the same death-wish as that displayed by Mr. Yacub, the mad scientist who attempted to bleach blackness (good) out of the race through a controlled program of mate selection, in order to create a white (evil) race.

Certainly we agree with Cleaver in his implication that the severance of the black man from his African heritage was one of the most dastardly crimes ever perpetuated by the white man in the history of this republic. And the black man's adoption of the dominant European culture is equally abominable. But Cleaver's rejection of Baldwin on these grounds reflects a gross violation of the truth and honesty of the situation. In the first place, the reality of the cultural predicament of the black man in America during the 1930s when Baldwin was growing up in Harlem was that African culture was virtually inaccessible to all blacks. As a result, there was a mass adoption of white culture by black people, by virtue of the fact that they were unable to identify with the culture of Africa. And the black literary tradition is replete with documentation of this unfortunate fact. Thus, to condemn Baldwin is to reject that entire tradition from James Weldon Johnson (*Autobiography of an Ex-Colored Man*) to Malcolm X (*Autobiography of Malcolm X*). Moreover, Cleaver's own admission that he once lusted for white women clearly illustrates this point. The argument also breaks down on another level. When we consider that its cogency depends in part upon the juxtaposition of the culture issue and the Yacub myth, it becomes obvious that, simultaneously, Cleaver has transferred

Yacub's attitude to Baldwin, and he has sprung the reader-trap of condemning Baldwin by virtue of the ideological association that Cleaver *assumes* him to have had with the perfidious deeds of the mad scientist.

## II "*The Literary Ghetto*"

The black militant assessment of Baldwin's writings, consequently, is drawn in purely negative terms. Cleaver concludes that his work "conceals [and] leads us away from . . . the most fundamental revolution which men have ever been called upon to make in their lives,"[7] and Baraka rejects not only Baldwin, but the entire black literary tradition as well.[8] These objections, beyond a doubt, have their foundation in self-serving efforts by Cleaver and Baraka to assert themselves by repudiating Baldwin because his artistic persuasions differ from theirs. But self-affirmation cannot be achieved through a rejection of Baldwin's literary contribution, as Calvin Hernton concludes:

> Let me make one thing absolutely clear. [Black writers on the current scene] are not in competition with James Baldwin, nor are they in conflict with him. Nor can anyone take Baldwin's "place" as a writer, and certainly not as a black writer. Baldwin is an individual writer in his own right. (All writers are individual writers in their own right.) The sooner this is recognized the sooner black writers will stop falling for the white man's trick of "Who's Going To Be Our Next Great Token Nigger Writer While the Rest of You Fight Among Yourselves!"[9]

Literary freedom, we must come to realize, is as vital to the artist as personal freedom is to his audience. Just as the reader must be free to accept or reject the artistic contribution, so the writer must be free to write what he must. And any attempt to abridge that freedom must be regarded as an intolerable invasion upon the sanctity of art. The effort must be made, at all costs, to insure the achievement of two objectives which need not become irreconcilable: the toleration of ideological diversity among black writers and the preservation of the Afro-American tradition in literature. Thus, the rejoinder that Cecil M. Brown makes in his response to Baraka's sweeping indictment of black literature is of momentous significance to those who would destroy in order to build: "Young Black writers should write whatever they feel impelled to write and let the labels fall where they may; at the same time, it is not

necessary to condemn the whole tradition of Afro-American
literature because it does not conform to what one happens to be
writing. No Black writer can write anything worthwhile without being influenced by writers—essentially blues writers—like Richard
Wright, James Baldwin, and James Weldon Johnson. And they need
not go around saying they can."[10]

Not only do these observations describe a serious pitfall which
black writers must strive to avoid, but they also reiterate the
"literary ghetto" concept which serves as a formidable impediment
to white critics, many of whom find themselves in sympathy with
this theory. As a result, these critics are inclined to employ one of
the most detrimental practices in evaluating black artistry: the
grouping and comparison of black writers for the purpose of
denigrating their art. In a classic demonstration of this syndrome,
Harvey Webster begins his 1953 review of *Go Tell* "by a brilliant
newcomer, James Baldwin":

In the early 1900's most novels by Negroes probably were unpublished;
those that were usually were cries of anger without measure or pleas for
condescension. In the years between 1920 and 1950, the best novels by
Negroes continued to emphasize either anger or compliance, but anyone
who read could see the immense gain in craft the novels of Arna Bontemps,
Langston Hughes, Chester Himes, and Richard Wright represented. In the
Fifties—with Wright's "The Outsider," with Ralph Ellison's "Invisible
Man," and now with James Baldwin's "Go Tell It on the Mountain"—the
Negro novel has finally come of age.[11]

Webster recounts, in one brief paragraph, a summation of the black
novel in the twentieth century. This is a gross oversimplification
because it assumes that the history of the black novel can be read in
terms of a series of lock-step progressions by black writers, who,
lacking individual persuasion and integrity, come to represent a
collective, unified group in pursuit of certain objectives which
Webster presumes to define. Lacking a horizontal ideological
dimension, the development of the black novel then becomes a
series of vertical movements in American literary history. Thus, we
begin with Bontemps at one end of the spectrum and end with the
emergence of Baldwin at the other.

Nearly twenty years later, this practice continues to undermine
the Afro-American literary tradition. In *Celebration in Postwar
American Fiction* (1970), Richard Rupp presents an updated version
of the ghetto in the chapter on Baldwin, which begins with "a study
in contrasts":

James Baldwin and Ralph Ellison present an interesting study in contrasts. Doubtless the best of our Negro writers, they demonstrate that "the Negro writer" is a myth. They differ in almost every significant respect: Baldwin is anguished, solemn, sublimely idealistic, and a little prissy. Ellison is Rabelaisian, funny, tough-minded, and awkward. Clearly Baldwin is a Paleface and Ellison is a Redskin, to use Philip Rahv's distinction. (LeRoi Jones, who qualifies as a real revolutionary, does not qualify as a serious writer.) But the most telling difference between Baldwin and Ellison is their attitude toward celebration. Festivity, present in Baldwin's early work, declines into hopelessness as his fiction develops, whereas Ellison, using a variety of tricks, styles, and modes, embraces the world with jokes and riotous laughter.[12]

Aside from the writings of Baldwin and Ellison, Rupp discusses "celebration" in the works of eight white writers. However, when he makes the study in contrasts, he chooses to analyze Baldwin's writings in conjunction with those of Ellison. Rupp summarily dismisses LeRoi Jones as a "serious" writer, declares a disbelief in the myth of "the Negro writer," and proclaims Baldwin and Ellison "the best of our Negro writers." Ironically, in denying recognition to other black twentieth-century writers, Rupp actually perpetuates the Negro-writer myth which he denounces, through his acceptance of the literary ghetto from which he allows only Ellison and Baldwin to emerge.

This grouping and comparison of black artists tends to be representative of a subtly masked form of racism which functions to stifle and suppress black talent and confirm the myth that blacks are limited in their capacity to produce serious literature. In his utter rejection of the ghetto fable, Edward Watson isolates three interrelated assumptions which contribute to the perpetuation of this *modus operandi:*

Several factors seem to lead to the grouping and comparison of Negro writers with each other, the primary one being the assumption that all novels written by Negroes are protests. . . . A second, related factor is the continuous refusal to judge works upon their artistic merit rather than on their social setting. Thirdly, there is a reluctance on the part of American critics to examine and relate the experiences of the novels of Negro authors to similar or related experiences in other novels on the moral, esthetic and technical planes.[13]

### III  *Protest Literature: Denial and Rejection*

The term "protest literature" (and all of the subtle connotative allusions to the Afro-American literary tradition) can only be un-

derstood in its full breadth and scope when it is considered in relation to the mainstream of American literature. The changing
character of life in the United States since the end of the Civil War
has afforded many opportunities for the satirization of American
customs and traditions, among which were the encroachment of
materialism, the advent of mechanization, and the evils of slavery.
As a result, mainstream American literature is replete with "protest
literature." Let us consider just a few examples.

Mark Twain's *The Gilded Age*, published in 1873, criticized
America as a land of corruption where new entrepeneurs
—Carnegie, Sumner, and Rockefeller—had led the nation
into an era of getting and spending as the source of happiness.
The loss of the dignity and virtue of the common man in our scuffle
for material wealth was lamented in *Leaves of Grass*, and in this
work also Walt Whitman issued a scathing condemnation of
traditional concepts of love and sexuality. Moreover, the poetry of
Robert Frost is remonstrative in the sense that it places a renewed
emphasis on the closeness of man to nature at a time when modern
technology threatened to engulf the simple values of the world of
nature. The poems "Revelation" and "Mending Wall," typical examples of Frost's protest, turn a sharp, critical eye on the barriers
that men continually erect to understanding and communication. In
*An American Tragedy* and *Sister Carrie,* Theodore Dreiser sought
to expose the corruptive influence of money and power which led to
the discrepancy between the American Ethic and the ruthless reality of the American Dream. Sinclair Lewis presents in *Babbitt* a por-
trait of an intellectually sterile society whose values dictate that
human communication transpire on the level of dehumanized con-
vention. In *Long Day's Journey into Night* and *Desire Under the
Elms*, Eugene O'Neill probes into the rampant corruption attendant
to the devotion to materialism, and in *The American Dream* and
*The Zoo Story*, Edward Albee satirizes the disintegration of
American society and the injustices of the American way of life
which become a deterrent to human intercourse and interaction.

Theoretically, some of the greatest literature written by white artists in the twentieth century takes its place in the protest tradition.
And while the denotation of the term "protest" suggests an impar-
tial application to white and black writers alike, the connotative
assumptions which we have come to make suggest that it is a
designation reserved for literature written by black Americans, all of
which is assumed to be a remonstration against the economic,

social, and political condition of the black man in America. As a descriptive phrase, it becomes a literary innuendo which proclaims the inferiority and sterility of the Afro-American literary tradition. The question is why white society finds it necessary to use this means of condemning black writing. Why does the white psyche thrive upon the denial of black literary efforts? Hoyt W. Fuller, in pondering these questions and analyzing this situation, arrives at a tenable explanation:

> . . . Negro literature is dismissed as "protest literature" because, if it deals honestly with Negro life, it will be accusatory toward white people, and nobody likes to be accused, especially of crimes against the human spirit. The reading public must realize, then, that while it is the duty of any serious writer to look critically and truthfully at the society of which he is a part, and to reveal that society to itself, the Negro writer, by virtue of his identification with a group deliberately held on the outer edges of that society, will, if he is honest, call attention to that special aspect of the society's failure.[14]

The problem here is that whites are unable to come to terms with reality, and therefore, they refuse to accept or confront the depressing social conditions to which black writers call attention. Consequently, the accusations contained in the literature can be brushed aside, and the issue of the failure of society can be bypassed. This releases whites from the necessity of justifying the mass exclusion of blacks from participation in the great American Dream.

## IV    Touchstones of the Sixties:
### Social Commentary Versus Artistic Creation

The inherent danger in assessing the contributions of a writer while he lives is further complicated, in Baldwin's case, by the fact that he is a black writer in a society which is dominated by the literature (and the criticism) of white Americans. Hence, much of the assessment of the Sixties, like the criticism of the essays upon which the assessments rest, is viewed sociologically. An excellent example of this situation is the evaluation of Baldwin's writings which is made by Beau Fly Jones, as follows:

> . . . perhaps the most useful aspect of Baldwin's writings is his understanding of the special problems created for Negroes by whites. He was one of the first writers to define extensively the details of what it is like to

be a Negro in a white society. He is one of the only Negro writers to portray such a wide range of Negro characters in his fiction; to discuss with such insight the psychological handicaps that most Negroes must face; and to realize the complexities of Negro-white relations in so many different contexts. . . .

Baldwin's most outstanding triumph is, however, a personal one. He has made a great contribution to the identity of his race, his nation and his profession—mainly because what he says rings true. In re-defining what has been called the Negro problem as white, he has forced the majority race in America to look at the damage it has done, and its own role in that destruction. . . .[15]

The major hypothesis explored in Chapter 5 is that Baldwin's writings have validity within both the social and the artistic contexts. Consequently, the singular objection to Jones's appraisal is that he has clearly confused Baldwin's social contributions with his artistic legacy. He begins in paragraph one by discussing "the most useful aspect of Baldwin's writing," and we are led to believe that this is an artistic venture. But instead, we get pure sociology. In the second paragraph, we get "Baldwin's most outstanding triumph, . . ." followed again by a sociological evaluation. I have cited Jones's comments because of their value as social commentary, but we must not fall into the literary trap of accepting them for anything that approaches the artistic.

Edward Watson reaches the common conclusion that Baldwin's achievement as an artist lies in his essays. But, unlike most critics, he presents us with an artistic basic for this judgment:

Baldwin, more than any other contemporary American writer, has worked consistently well with the essay as a particular form of literary expression. He has shown what can be done with the essay and how effective is its form to incorporate personal conviction on a variety of subjects. Despite the popularity of the novel today, Baldwin has reminded us that non-fictional works are always an integral part of any country's literature. Whether he will be remembered as an essayist or a novelist is not the great question; the question is, what more is needed for a Negro to be included in "the central community of American letters" . . . ?[16]

It is reassuring to discover critics like Watson who are willing to weigh Baldwin's writings on the scale of serious literature and begin the journey beyond the superficialities of thematic and categorizing labels to discover Baldwin's talent and artistry.

Another effort in this direction is made by Therman B. O'Daniel in a rather comprehensive evaluation of Baldwin's work. In the first place, O'Daniel argues, Baldwin has achieved "phenomenal success" as a writer because

> he is the gifted possessor of that primary element, genuine talent. . . . Secondly, he is a very intelligent and deeply perceptive observer of our multifarious contemporary society. . . . In the third place, Baldwin is a bold and courageous writer who is not afraid to search into the dark corners of our social consciences, and to force out into public view many of the hidden, sordid skeletons of our society. . . . Then, of course, there is Baldwin's literary style which is a fourth major reason for his success as a writer. His prose . . . possesses a crystal clearness and a passionately poetic rhythm that makes it most appealing. . . . Finally, James Baldwin . . . employs . . . more than one of the prose types and several of the communication mediums—the magazine, the newspapers, and the printed book—to keep his voice heard and his pen alive.[17]

## V   *Trends of the Seventies: Toward Universal Dimensions*

The critical stance exemplified by Watson and O'Daniel gives us a prophetic insight into the present decade. The advent of the Seventies ushered in a shift in the critical perspective which characterized the evaluation of Baldwin's art during the Sixties. As the emotional heat of the civil rights era began to diminish, many critics sought to reject the narrow context of sociology as a primary consideration in their judgment of Baldwin's writings. The trend points toward a broader, more comprehensive evaluation of the artistic style and the human concerns which constitute a more fundamental aspect of the Baldwin legacy. Thus we entered that era which Wordsworth so artfully described as "emotion in tranquility recollected."

One of the typical critical assessments during this period is Karin Moller's full length study of the theme of identity in Baldwin's essays. Here Professor Moller strikes a note of universality as she discusses *Notes of a Native Son, Nobody Knows My Name, The Fire Next Time, Nothing Personal,* and *No Name in the Street* with an emphasis on the Edenic Fall of man, Christian versus Satanic images, man as a beneficiary of evil, and the human effort to distinguish between the moral forces of good and evil. She concludes that, for Baldwin, the concept of identity is not limited to white or black. Most basic to all of his discussions concerning identity is the concept of *human identity,* which is:

equivalent to a spiritual maturity that implies full consciousness of all kinds of dualities which may be problematic for men to handle. (Among such difficult contrasts which human beings must somehow learn to live with are those of life-death, good-evil, and childhood-maturity). To be able to live with a sense of the complication of the predicament thus created for man is a sign of maturity attained, of "identity" achieved. This is the same for *all* men, African and American, black and white.[18]

The same position is maintained by critic Fred L. Standley in his recent discussion of *Another Country*. Standley initiates a scholarly consideration of the structural, symbolic, and thematic bases of the novel, and he analyzes the title in terms which support Professor Moller's conclusions concerning Baldwin's concept of the idea of identity:

Philosophically, "another country" suggests the American escapism that denies the reality of pain and suffering and tragedy, and the necessity to learn to live under and with them, which is the essence of "the blues" indigenous to the blacks in America. The voice of Bessie Smith singing in the background . . . keeps this leitmotif present and moves the novel into the universal predicament for man, that is, learning to confront the tragic.[19]

The achievement of identity, then, suggests an acceptance of the dualities of life as well as the development of a strategy for confronting the realities of our existence.

Another scholar-teacher-critic whose writing deserves consideration is Shirley S. Allen.[20] In her analysis of *Go Tell It on the Mountain*, Professor Allen emphasizes the "human concern" as she views the tension in the novel from the perspective of a *Bildungsroman*. Although she finds literary parallels in the writings of Dickens, Dostoevski, and Hawthorne, the chief value of her work lies in the extended and illuminating discussion of the biblical symbolism which Baldwin employs. This trend in serious criticism is also reflected in John Fleischauer's discussion of Baldwin's style.[21] Fleischauer explains his method of using Baldwin's technique as a model for his students, and he pursues the manifestations of the style as a reflection of the "uniqueness of the man" who is part of the "universal tradition" which speaks to "universal man."

The significance of the work of these representative critics is that it is permeated by an objective perception which searches beyond Baldwin as social commentator to call attention to his status as a writer in twentieth century America and to link him with other writers on a universal plane. Over the past twenty-five years, Baldwin has carved a literary niche through his exploration of "the mystery of the human being" in his art. His short stories, novels, and plays shed the light of reality upon the darkness of our illusions, while the essays bring a boldness, courage, and cool logic to bear on the most crucial questions of humanity with which this country has yet to be faced. Indeed, the unusually striking metaphors and similes, the precisely balanced sentences, the poetic rhythm and diction, the lucidity of the prose, the striking catalogs, and the technique of juxtaposing physical and psychological deprivation, all testify to the brilliant achievement of James Baldwin, artist and "incorrigible disturber of the peace."

Baldwin's artistry not only documents the dilemma of the black man in American society, but it also bears witness to the struggle of the artist against the overwhelming forces of oppression. Almost invariably, his protagonists are artists: Luke and David *(The Amen Corner)*, Rufus *(Another Country)*, Richard *(Blues for Mister Charlie)*, and Sonny ("Sonny's Blues") are all musicians. Leo Proudhammer *(Tell Me How Long the Train's Been Gone)* and Peter ("Previous Condition") are both actors. The narrator-artist in "This Morning, This Evening, So Soon" has established his reputation as a singer, and Fonny is an aspiring sculptor in *If Beale Street Could Talk*. Each character is engaged in the pursuit of artistic fulfillment which, for Baldwin, becomes symbolic of the quest for identity.

As contemporaries of Baldwin, we are unable to assess the impact that his writings will have on posterity because we lack the retrospective tranquility necessary in order to view them objectively. Yet historical and literary precedent seems to suggest that the final judgments may be linked to his ability to analyze the black experience for its universal dimensions. Baldwin has sought to use that experience as a means of joining hands with humanity, with the universal brotherhood of mankind, and this effort may prove to be his ultimate triumph and distinction, as William Smart observes:

Those [works of art] which survive do so because they manage to transcend the purely temporal aspects of their subjects, they reveal problems—relationships between people—that exist from generation to generation and from nation to nation. Thus, if an essay such as "Notes of a Native Son" lasts beyond our own time, it will most likely be not because of what it tells us about Negro-white relations, but, rather, for what it says about the relationship between a certain father and son.[22]

Baldwin's works, then, like those of other writers, must be subjected to the ebb and flow of the literary tide through the course of history. And perhaps in the future, as we discover the freedom to reject the restricting label of "protest," we can intensify our efforts to come to terms with Baldwin's legacy in order to delve beneath the message of his writings and apprehend the consummate artistic skill which transcends the social value of his artistry.

# Notes and References

## Chapter One

1. Fern Marja Eckman, *The Furious Passage of James Baldwin* (New York: M. Evans, 1966), p. 11.

2. James Baldwin, "Disturber of the Peace: James Baldwin" (an interview by Eve Auchincloss and Nancy Lynch), *Mademoiselle*, May 1963; rpt. in *The Black American Writer*, Vol. I, ed. C. W. E. Bigsby (Baltimore: Penguin Books, 1971), p. 212.

3. Louis Phillips, "LeRoi Jones and Contemporary Black Drama," *The Black American Writer*, Vol. II, p. 205.

4. Jane Howard, " 'Doom and Glory of Knowing Who You Are' " (an interview with James Baldwin), *Life*, May 24, 1963, p. 90.

5. Seymour Krim, "The Troubles He's Seen," review of *Going to Meet the Man, Book Week*, November 7, 1965, p. 5.

6. Ben Shahn, Darius Milhaud, and James Baldwin, "The Image: Three Views" (comments from a symposium at Hofstra College, May 1961), *Opera News*, 27 (December 8, 1962), 12.

7. James Baldwin, "Autobiographical Notes," *Notes of a Native Son* (Boston: Beacon Press, 1955; New York: Bantam Books, 1968), p. 2. All quotations from this collection of essays are from this edition, hereafter cited as *Notes*.

8. Eckman, *Furious Passage*, p. 242.

9. Ibid., p. 158.

10. James Baldwin, *Nobody Knows My Name* (New York: Dial Press, 1961; New York: Dell Publishing Company, 1970), p. 18. All quotations from this collection of essays are from this edition, hereafter cited as *Nobody*.

11. James Baldwin, "As Much Truth As One Can Bear," *New York Times Book Review*, January 14, 1962, sec. 7, part 1, p. 1.

12. James Baldwin, "Mass Culture and the Creative Artist: Some Personal Notes," *Daedalus*, 89 (Spring 1960), 375 - 76.

13. Ibid., p. 373.

14. Howard, " 'Doom and Glory'," p. 89.

15. "As Much Truth," p. 38.

16. "The Black Boy Looks at the White Boy," *Nobody*, pp. 187 - 88.

17. Ben Shahn, et. al. "The Image," p. 9.

18. James Baldwin, Colin MacInnes, and James Mossman, "Race, Hate, Sex, and Colour: A Conversation," *Encounter*, 25 (July 1965), 56.

19. Richard Wright, "How Bigger Was Born," *Saturday Review*, June 1, 1940, p. 18.

20. Ibid., p. 19.

21. "Alas, Poor Richard," *Nobody,* p. 151.

22. Kichung Kim, "Wright, the Protest Novel, and Baldwin's Faith," *College Language Association Journal* (1974) 17: 394.

23. Eckman, *Furious Passage,* p. 24.

24. Imamu Amiri Baraka, "Nationalism Vs Pimp Art," *Raise Race Rays Raze: Essays Since 1965* (New York: Random House, 1971), p. 125.

25. LeRoi Jones [Imamu Amiri Baraka], "The Myth of a 'Negro Literature'," *Home: Social Essays* (New York: William Morrow, 1966), pp. 114 - 15.

26. Mike Coleman, "What Is Black Theater?" (An interview with Imamu Amiri Baraka), *Black World,* April 1971, p. 36.

27. Cecil M. Brown, "Black Literature and LeRoi Jones," *Black World,* June 1970, pp. 25 - 26.

28. Hoyt W. Fuller, "Contemporary Negro Fiction," *Southwest Review,* 50 (Autumn 1965), 327.

29. James Baldwin, "Down at the Cross," *The Fire Next Time* (New York: Dial Press, 1963; New York: Dell Publishing, 1972), pp. 57 - 58. All quotations from this collection of essays are from this edition, hereafter cited as *Fire.*

30. Ibid., p. 67.

31. Coleman, "Black Theater," p. 34.

32. Douglas Turner Ward, "American Theatre: For Whites Only?" *New York Times,* August 14, 1966, sec. 2, p. D-1.

33. Douglas Turner Ward, "The Goal is Autonomy," *New York Times,* February 2, 1969, sec. 2, p. D-9.

34. James Baldwin, "The Price May Be Too High," *New York Times,* February 2, 1969, sec. 2, p. D-9.

35. Ibid.

36. Sally Smith, "James Baldwin: The Expatriate Becomes Disillusioned," *Atlanta Constitution,* May 19, 1976, p. 21.

37. Jewell Handy Gresham, "James Baldwin Comes Home," *Essence,* June 1976, p. 55.

38. James Baldwin, *The Devil Finds Work* (New York: Dial Press, 1976), pp. 16 - 17. All quotations from this collection of essays are from this edition, hereafter cited as *Devil.*

39. John A. Williams, "Problems of the Negro Writer: The Literary Ghetto," *Saturday Review,* April 20, 1963, p. 21.

### Chapter Two

1. Fred L. Standley, "James Baldwin: The Crucial Situation," *South Atlantic Quarterly,* 65 (Summer 1966), 373.

2. Carl Michalson, *Faith for Personal Crises* (New York: Scribner's, 1958), pp. 5 - 137 passim.

3. James Baldwin, *Going to Meet the Man* (New York: Dial Press, 1965;

New York: Dell Publishing 1971), p. 86. Page references are given in parentheses following the quotation.

4. James Baldwin and Nikki Giovanni, *A Dialogue* (Philadelphia: J. B. Lippincott, 1973), p. 17.

5. "Many Thousands Gone," *Notes*, p. 33.

6. James Baldwin et al., "Liberalism and the Negro: A Round Table Discussion," *Commentary*, 37 (March 1964), 35.

7. Ibid., p. 36.

8. Ibid., p. 37.

9. Sam Bluefarb, "James Baldwin's 'Previous Condition': A Problem of Identification," *Negro American Literature Forum*, 3 (Spring 1969), 27.

10. Ibid., p. 28.

11. "The Discovery of What It Means to Be an American," *Nobody*, p. 17.

12. Ibid., p. 20.

13. Joseph W. Vollmerhausen, "Alienation in the Light of Horney's Theory of Neurosis," *The American Journal of Psychoanalysis*, 21 (1961), 147 - 48.

14. William H. Grier and Price M. Cobbs, *Black Rage* (New York: Basic Books, 1968; New York: Bantam Books, Inc., 1969), p. 7.

15. Dexter M. Bullard, ed. "Psychiatric Aspects of Anxiety," *Psychoanalysis and Psychotherapy: Selected Papers of Frieda Fromm-Reichmann* (Chicago: University of Chicago Press, 1959; Chicago: University of Chicago Press, 1960), p. 311.

16. James Baldwin et al., "The Negro in American Culture," *Cross Currents*, 11 (Spring 1961), 215.

17. Ibid.

18. *Social Theory and Social Structure* (Glencoe, Illinois: The Free Press, 1957), p. 128. Quoted in Beau Fly Jones, "James Baldwin: The Struggle for Identity," *The British Journal of Sociology* 17 (June 1966), 109.

## Chapter Three

1. James Baldwin, *Go Tell It on the Mountain* (London: Michael Joseph, 1954; New York: Dell Publishing Company, 1972). All quotations from this novel are from this edition, hereafter cited as *Go Tell*. Page references are given in parentheses following the quotation.

2. "Introduction," *Nobody*, p 13.

3. Walt Whitman, "Starting from Paumanok," Verse 6, *Leaves of Grass*, ed. Sculley Bradley (New York: Rinehart, 1958), p. 15.

4. *A Dialogue*, p. 80.

5. Robert K. Bingham and Gouveneur Paulding, "Two American Writers," review of *Go Tell It on the Mountain* by James Baldwin and *Letters of Sherwood Anderson* by Sherwood Anderson, *The Reporter*, VIII (June 23, 1953), 38 - 39.

6. "The Northern Protestant," *Nobody*, p. 140.

7. Stanley Macebuh, *James Baldwin: A Critical Study* (New York: The Third Press, 1973), p. 62.

8. James Baldwin, *Giovanni's Room* (New York: Dial Press, 1956; New York: Dell Publishing, 1969). All quotations from this novel are from this edition. Page references are given in parentheses following the quotation.

9. Henry James, "The Art of Fiction," *American Literature: Tradition and Innovation*, Vol. 2, ed. Harrison T. Meserole et al. (Lexington, Massachusetts: D. C. Heath , 1969), pp. 2632 - 2642 passim.

10. Eldridge Cleaver, "Notes on a Native Son," *Soul on Ice* (New York: McGraw-Hill, 1968), p. 110.

11. "Disturber of the Peace," pp. 213 - 14.

12. James Baldwin, *Another Country* (New York: Dial Press, 1962; New York: Dell Publishing, 1968). All quotations from this novel are from this edition. Page references are given in parentheses following the quotation.

13. "Liberalism and the Negro," p. 32.

14. Ibid.

15. James Baldwin, *Tell Me How Long the Train's Been Gone* (New York: Dial Press, 1968; New York: Dell Publishing, 1972). All quotations from this novel are from this edition, hereafter cited as *Tell Me*. Page references are given in parentheses following the quotation.

16. Irving Howe, "James Baldwin: At Ease in Apocalypse," review of *Tell Me How Long the Train's Been Gone*, in *Harper's*, September 1968, pp. 96 - 97.

17. Ibid., p. 96.

18. Calvin C. Hernton, "Blood of the Lamb: The Ordeal of James Baldwin," *Amistad 1*, ed. John A. Williams and Charles F. Harris (DeLand, Florida: Everett Edwards, Inc., 1969; New York: Random House, Vintage Imprint, 1970), p. 210.

19. James Baldwin, *If Beale Street Could Talk* (New York: The Dial Press, 1974). All quotations from this novel, hereafter cited as *If Beale Street*, are from this edition. Page references are given in parentheses following the quotation.

20. Grier and Cobbs, *Black Rage*, p. 68.

## Chapter Four

1. James Baldwin, "The Creative Dilemma," *Saturday Review*, February 8, 1964, pp. 14 - 15.

2. James Baldwin, *The Amen Corner* (New York: The Dial Press, 1968). All quotations from this play are from this edition, hereafter cited as *Amen*. Page references are given in parentheses following the quotation.

3. Standley, "James Baldwin: The Crucial Situation," pp. 375 - 76.

4. James Baldwin, *Blues for Mister Charlie* (New York: Dial Press; New York: Dell Publishing Company, 1964). All quotations from this play are from this edition, hereafter cited as *Blues*. Page references are given in parentheses following the quotation.

5. Louis Phillips, "The Novelist as Playwright: Baldwin, McCullers, and Bellow," *Modern American Drama: Essays and Criticism*, ed. William E. Taylor (DeLand, Florida: Everett Edwards, Inc., 1968), p. 147.

6. James Baldwin, "The American Dream and the American Negro," *New York Times Magazine*, March 7, 1965, p. 33.

7. "Disturber of the Peace," p. 200.

8. "Down at the Cross," *Fire*, p. 47.

9. Ibid., p. 40.

10. James Baldwin, *One Day, When I Was Lost* (London: Michael Joseph, 1972; rpt. New York: Dial Press, 1973). All quotations from this play are from this edition, hereafter cited as *One Day*. Page references are given in parentheses following the quotation.

11. C. Eric Lincoln, *The Black Muslims in America* (Boston: Beacon Press, 1961), p. 248.

12. "Notes for *Blues*," *Blues*, p. 8.

### Chapter Five

1. Irving Howe, "Black Boys and Native Sons," *A World More Attractive* (New York: Horizon Press, 1963), p. 120.

2. David Levin, "Baldwin's Autobiographical Essays: The Problem of Negro Identity," *Massachusetts Review*, 5 (Winter 1964), 239.

3. Augusta Strong, "Notes on James Baldwin," *Freedomways*, 2 (Spring 1962), 168.

4. Edward A. Watson, "The Novels and Essays of James Baldwin: Casebook of a 'Lover's War' with the United States," *Queen's Quarterly* 72 (Summer 1965), 399.

5. Robert Donald Spector, "Everybody Knows His Name," review of *Another Country*, *New York Herald Tribune Books*, June 17, 1962, sec. 6, p. 3.

6. Nat Hentoff, " 'It's Terrifying'," *New York Herald Tribune Books*, June 16, 1963, sec. 6, pp. 5 - 6.

7. James Baldwin in "James Baldwin" (an interview by John Hall), *The Transatlantic Review*, 37 / 38 (Autumn-Winter 1970 - 71), 6.

8. Howard Levant, "Aspiraling We Should Go," *Midcontinent American Studies Journal*, 4 (Fall 1963), 15.

9. Ibid.

10. "Fifth Avenue, Uptown," *Nobody Knows My Name*. Page references from this essay collection, hereafter cited as *Nobody*, are given in parentheses following the quotation.

11. James Baldwin, *No Name in the Street* (New York: Dial Press, 1972), p. 149. All quotations from this collection of essays are from this edition, hereafter cited as *No Name*. Page references are given in parentheses following the quotation.

12. "Down at the Cross," *The Fire Next Time*, p. 33. Page references from this work are given in parentheses following the quotation.

13. Richard H. Rupp, *Celebration in Postwar American Fiction: 1945 - 1967* (Coral Gables, Florida: University of Miami Press, 1970), pp. 222 - 23.

14. *Notes.* Page references from this collection of essays, are given in parentheses following the quotation.

15. James Baldwin and Margaret Mead, *A Rap on Race* (Philadelphia: J. B. Lippincott, 1971). All quotations from this dialogue are from this edition, hereafter cited as *Rap.* Page references are given in parentheses following the quotation.

16. *A Dialogue.* Page references from this work are given in parentheses following the quotation.

## Chapter Six

1. LeRoi Jones, "Brief Reflections on Two Hot Shots," *Home: Social Essays*, p. 120.

2. Cleaver, "Notes on a Native Son," p. 99.

3. Jervis Anderson, "Race, Rage and Eldridge Cleaver," review of *Soul on Ice* by Eldridge Cleaver, *Commentary*, 41 (December 1968), 67 - 68.

4. Julian Mayfield, "The New Mainstream," review of *Soul on Ice* by Eldridge Cleaver, *Nation*, May 13, 1968, p. 638.

5. Addison Gayle, "A Defense of James Baldwin," *College Language Association Journal*, 10 (March 1967), 207.

6. Cleaver, "Notes on a Native Son," p. 106 - 108.

7. Ibid., p. 110.

8. See LeRoi Jones, "The Myth of a 'Negro Literature'," *Home*, pp. 105 - 115.

9. Hernton, "Blood of the Lamb," p. 213.

10. Brown, "Black Literature," p. 31.

11. Harvey Curtis Webster, "Community of Pride," review of *Go Tell It on the Mountain, Saturday Review*, May 16, 1953, p. 14.

12. Rupp, *Celebration*, p. 133.

13. Watson, "Novels and Essays," p. 400.

14. Fuller, "Negro Fiction," p. 324.

15. Beau Fly Jones, "Struggle for Identity," p. 119.

16. Watson, "Novels and Essays," p. 401.

17. Therman B. O'Daniel, "James Baldwin: An Interpretative Study," *College Language Association Journal* 7 (September 1963), 37 - 38.

18. Karin Moller, *The Theme of Identity in the Essays of James Baldwin: An Interpretation*, Gothenburg Studies in English 32 (Goteberg, Sweden: Acta Universitatis Gothoburgensis, 1975), p. 63.

19. Fred L. Standley, "Another Country, Another Time," *Studies in the Novel*, 4 (Fall, 1972), p. 508.

20. Shirley S. Allen, "Religious Symbolism and Psychic Reality in

Baldwin's *Go Tell It on the Mountain,"* *College Language Association Journal,* 19 (December, 1975).

21. John Fleischauer, "James Baldwin's Style: A Prospectus for the Classroom," *College Composition and Communication* 26 (1975).

22. William Smart, "James Baldwin," *Eight Modern Essayists* (New York: St. Martins Press, 1965), p. 299.

# Selected Bibliography

PRIMARY SOURCES

(Listed Chronologically)

A.  Novels and Collected Short Stories

*Go Tell It on the Mountain*. London: Michael Joseph, 1954. Page references in the text are to the Dell Publishing Company edition, 6th printing, August, 1972.

*Giovanni's Room*. New York: Dial Press, 1956. Page references in the text are to the Dell Publishing Company edition, 9th printing, November, 1969.

*Another Country*. New York: Dial Press, 1962. Page references in the text are to the Dell Publishing Company edition, 16th printing, March, 1968.

*Going to Meet the Man*. New York: Dial Press 1965. Page references in the text are to the Dell Publishing Company edition, 8th printing, March, 1971.

*Tell Me How Long the Train's Been Gone*. New York: Dial Press, 1968. Page references in the text are to the Dell Publishing Company edition, 6th printing, April, 1972.

*If Beale Street Could Talk*. New York: Dial Press, 1974.


B.  Plays

*Blues for Mister Charlie*. New York: Dial Press, 1964. Page references in the text are to the Dell Publishing Company edition, 1st printing, November, 1964.

*The Amen Corner*. New York: Dial Press, 1968.

One Day, When I Was Lost. London: Michael Joseph, 1972. Page references in the text are to the Dial edition, 1973.


C.  Essays and Dialogues

*Notes of a Native Son*. Boston: Beacon Press, 1955. Page references in the text are to the Bantam Books edition, 6th printing, May, 1968.

*Nobody Knows My Name*. New York: Dial Press, 1961. Page references in the text are to the Dell Publishing Company edition, 15th printing, July, 1970.

*The First Next Time*. New York: Dial Press, 1963. Page references in the text are to the Dell Publishing Company edition, 3rd printing, October, 1972.

*A Rap on Race* (with Margaret Mead). Philadelphia: J. B. Lippincott, 1971.
*No Name in the Street.* New York: Dial Press, 1972.
*A Dialogue* (with Nikki Giovanni). Philadelphia: J. B. Lippincott, 1973.
*The Devil Finds Work.* New York: Dial Press, 1976.


D.    Uncollected Essays

"A Word from the Writer Directly to Reader." In *Fiction of the Fifties*, edited by Herbert Gold, pp. 18 - 19. New York: Doubleday, 1959.

"Mass Culture and the Creative Artist: Some Personal Notes." *Daedalus*, LXXXIX (Spring 1960), 373 - 76.

"They Can't Turn Back." *Mademoiselle*, LI (August 1960), 324.

"The Dangerous Road Before Martin Luther King." *Harper's*, CCXXII (February 1961), 33 - 42.

"As Much Truth As One Can Bear." *New York Times Book Review*, January 14, 1962, pt. 1, p. 1.

"Letters from a Journey." *Harper's*, CCXXVI (May 1963), 48 - 52.

"At the Root of the Negro Problem." *Time*, LXXXI (May 17, 1963), 26.

"There's a Bill Due That Has to be Paid." *Life*, LIV (May 24, 1963), 81.

"A Talk to Teachers." *Saturday Review*, XLVI (December 21, 1963), 42.

"The Creative Dilemma." *Saturday Review*, XCVII (February 8, 1964), 14.

"Theatre: The Negro In and Out of It." In *Beyond the Angry Black*, compiled by John A. Williams, pp. 3 - 10. New York: Cooper Square, 1966.

"A Report from Occupied Territory." *Nation*, CCIII (July 11, 1966), 39 - 43.

"Negroes Are Anti-Semitic Because They're Anti-White." *New York Times Magazine*, April 9, 1967, p. 26.

"Sidney Poitier." *Look* XXXII (July 23, 1968), 50.

"The Price May Be Too High." *New York Times*, February 2, 1969, sec. 2, p. D - 9.

"Sweet Lorraine." *Esquire* LXXII (November 1969), 138 - 40.

"Unnameable Objects, Unspeakable Crimes." In *Black on Black*, edited by Arnold Adoff, pp. 105 - 113. New York: P. F. Collier, 1970.

"In Search of a Basis for Mutual Understanding and Racial Harmony." In *The Nature of a Humane Society*, edited by H. Ober Hess, pp. 231 - 240. Philadelphia: Fortress Press, 1977.


E.    Interviews and Discussions

"The Negro in American Culture" (with Nat Hentoff, Alfred Kazin, Lorraine Hansberry, Emile Capouya, and Langston Hughes). *Cross Currents* XI (Spring 1961), 205 - 224.

"The Image: Three Views" (with Ben Shahn and Darius Milhaud). *Opera News* XXVII (December 8, 1962), 9 - 12.

"Disturber of the Peace: James Baldwin" (an interview with Eva Auchincloss and Nancy Lynch). *Mademoiselle*, May 1963; reprinted in *The Black American Writer*, ed. C. W. E. Bigsby, vol. 1, pp. 199 - 215. Baltimore: Penguin Books, 1971.

"A Conversation with James Baldwin" (interview with Kenneth B. Clark). *Freedomways* III (Summer 1963), 361 - 68.

"Liberalism and the Negro: A Round-Table Discussion" (with Nathan Glazer, Sidney Hook, and Gunnar Myrdal). *Commentary* XXXVII (March 1964), 25 - 42.

"The American Dream and the American Negro" (with James Buckley). *New York Times Magazine*, March 7, 1965, p. 32.

"Race, Hate, Sex, and Colour: A Conversation" (with Colin MacInnes and James Mossman). *Encounter* XXV (July 1965), 55 - 60.

"James Baldwin Breaks His Silence" (an interview with Cep Dergisi). *Atlas* XIII (March 1967), 47 - 49.

"How Can We Get The Black People to Cool It?" *Esquire* LXX (July 1968), 49.

"James Baldwin" (an interview with John Hall). *The Transatlantic Review* XXXVII - XXXVIII (Autumn-Winter 1970 - 71), 5 - 14.

"James Baldwin Comes Home" (interview with Jewell H. Gresham) *Essence*, June 1976, p. 55ff.

SECONDARY SOURCES

A. Bibliographies

FISHER, RUSSELL G. "James Baldwin: A Bibliography, 1947 - 1962." *Bulletin of Bibliography* XXIV (1965), 127 - 30.

KINDT, KATHLEEN A. "James Baldwin: A Checklist: 1947 - 1962." *Bulletin of Bibliography* XXIV (1965), 123 - 26.

STANDLEY, FRED L. "James Baldwin: A Checklist: 1963 - 1967." *Bulletin of Bibliography* XXV (May - August 1968), 135ff.

B. Books

BARAKA, IMAMU AMIRI [LEROI JONES]. "Nationalism Vs. Pimp Art" in *Raise Race Rays Raze: Essays Since 1965*, pp. 125 - 32. New York: Random House, 1971. Defines Black Art as a vehicle for elevating the level of ethnic pride.

BULLARD, DEXTER M., ed. "Psychiatric Aspects of Anxiety" in *Psychoanalysis and Psychotherapy: Selected Papers of Frieda Fromm-Riechmann*. Chicago: University of Chicago Press, 1959; reprint Chicago: University of Chicago Press, 1960, pp. 306 - 321. Discusses anxiety as a basic factor in self-realization.

CLEAVER, ELDRIDGE. "Notes on a Native Son" in *Soul on Ice*, pp. 97 - 111. New York: McGraw-Hill, 1968. Takes Baldwin to task for his criticism of Richard Wright.

ECKMAN, FERN MARJA. *The Furious Passage of James Baldwin*. New York: M. Evans, 1966. Provides brief, but valuable insight into Baldwin's artistic theory.

GRIER, WILLIAM H. and PRICE M. COBBS. *Black Rage*. New York: Basic Books, 1968; New York: Bantam Books, Inc., 1969. Discussions, supported by case histories, of the psychiatric effects of racism on the black man in America.

HERNTON, CALVIN C. "Blood of the Lamb: The Ordeal of James Baldwin" in *Amistad 1: Writings on Black History and Culture*. Edited by John A. Williams and Charles F. Harris. DeLand, Florida: Everett Edwards, Inc., 1969; New York: Random House, 1970, pp. 183 - 225. Considers Baldwin's writings in contrast to those of the Black Arts Movement.

HOWE, IRVING. "Black Boys and Native Sons" in *A World More Attractive*, pp. 98 - 122. New York: Horizon Press, 1963. Defends Richard Wright against Baldwin's attack on *Native Son*.

JAMES, HENRY. "The Art of Fiction" in *American Literature: Tradition and Innovation*. Edited by Harrison T. Meserole, Walter Sutton, and Brom Weber. Vol. 2, pp. 2625 - 2642. Lexington, Massachusetts: D. C. Heath, 1969. Discusses the aims of art and the responsibilities of the artist.

JONES, LEROI. "Brief Reflections on Two Hot Shots" in *Home: Social Essays*, pp. 116 - 120. New York: William Morrow, 1966. Criticizes Baldwin and Peter Abraham for their unwillingness to become actively involved in the racial struggle.

———. "The Myth of a 'Negro Literature' " in *Home: Social Essays*, pp. 105 - 115. New York: William Morrow, 1966. Argues that no black literature exists because black writers have always imitated white writers.

KENT, GEORGE E. "Baldwin and the Problem of Being" in *Five Black Writers: Essays on Wright, Ellison, Baldwin, Hughes, and LeRoi Jones*, pp. 148 - 58. Edited by Donald R. Gibson. New York: New York University Press, 1970. Views the themes of sex and love as vehicles for the achievement of identity.

KINNAMON, KENNETH. *James Baldwin: A Collection of Critical Essays*. Englewood Cliffs, New Jersey: Prentice-Hall, 1974. Chronological grouping of essays written between 1956 and 1972 which discuss Baldwin's literary career as well as the themes and social implications in his work.

LINCOLN, C. ERIC. *The Black Muslims in America*. Boston: Beacon Press, 1961. An in-depth study of the origin, ideology, organizational structure, methods, and techniques of the Black Muslim Movement in America.

MACEBUH, STANLEY. *James Baldwin: A Critical Study*. New York: Joseph Okpaku Publishing, 1973. Attempts to examine Baldwin both as man and artist.

MICHALSON, CARL. *Faith for Personal Crises*. New York: Scribner, 1958. Uses the Christian perspective in discussing seven crises that individuals face in life.

MOLLER, KARIN. *The Theme of Identity in the Essays of James Baldwin; An Interpretation*. Gothenburg Studies in English 32. Goteborg Sweden: Acta Universitatis Gothoburgensis, 1975. Discussion of the quest for identity as a human concern in the collected essays from *Notes of a Native Son* to *No Name in the Street*.

PHILLIPS, LOUIS. "LeRoi Jones and Contemporary Black Drama" in *The Black American Writer*. Edited by C. W. E. Bigsby. Vol. 2, pp. 203 - 17. Deland, Florida: Everett Edwards, 1969; Baltimore: Penguin Books, 1971. Discusses the plays of LeRoi Jones in relation to the Black Arts Movement.

_____. "The Novelist as Playwright: Baldwin, McCullers, and Bellow" in *Modern American Drama: Essays in Criticism*, pp. 145 - 62. Edited by William E. Taylor. DeLand, Florida: Everett Edwards, 1968. Commentary on the theme of racial inequality and injustice in *Blues for Mister Charlie*.

RUPP, RICHARD H. "James Baldwin: The Search for Celebration" in *Celebration in Postwar American Fiction: 1945 - 1967*, pp. 133 - 149. Coral Gables, Florida: University of Miami Press, 1970. Discusses the dichotomy between Baldwin's vision and his fictional depiction of reality.

SMART, WILLIAM. "James Baldwin" in *Eight Modern Essayists*, pp. 298 - 300. New York: St. Martin's Press, 1965. Brief sketch, primarily biographical.

WHITMAN, WALT. "Starting from Paumanok." Verse 6. *Leaves of Grass*, pp. 11 - 23. Edited by Sculley Bradley. New York: Rinehart, 1958. Reflects Whitman's strong sense of nationalism.

C   Articles and Book Reviews

ALLEN, SHIRLEY S. "Religious Symbolism and Psychic Reality in Baldwin's *Go Tell It on the Mountain*." *College Language Association Journal* 19 (December 1975) 173 - 199. Extended analysis of the Biblical imagery and parallels.

ANDERSON, JERVIS. "Race, Rage and Eldridge Cleaver." Review of *Soul on Ice* by Eldridge Cleaver. *Commentary*, December 1968, pp. 63 - 69. Sharply critical of Cleaver's attack on Baldwin.

BELL, GEORGE E. "The Dilemma of Life in *Go Tell It on the Mountain* and *Giovanni's Room*." *College Language Association Journal* 17 (March 1974) 397 - 406. Discusses the theological and psychological pitfalls which block the path to love.

BINGHAM, ROBERT K. and GOUVENEUR PAULDING. "Two American Writers." Reviews of *Go Tell It on the Mountain* by James Baldwin and *Letters of Sherwood Anderson* by Sherwood Anderson. *The Reporter*, VIII (June 23, 1953), 38 - 39. Views Baldwin's novel as a search into the past.

BLUEFARB, SAM. "James Baldwin's 'Previous Condition': A Problem of Identification." *Negro American Literature Forum* 3 (Spring 1969), 26 - 29. An analysis of the dilemma which Peter faces as a black intellectual.

BROWN, CECIL M. "Black Literature and LeRoi Jones." *Black World*, June

1970, pp. 24 - 31. Refutes LeRoi Jones' argument that there is no black literature.

COLEMAN, MIKE. "What is Black Theater?" An interview with Amiri Baraka, *Black World*, April 1971, pp. 32-36. Discusses Black Theater as a movement, free from the financial dependence and the critical judgment of white society.

COLES, ROBERT. "James Baldwin Back Home." *New York Times Book Review*, July 31, 1977, p 1 ff. Brief but comprehensive discussion on Baldwin's views on American and world affairs.

FLEISCHAUER, JOHN F. "James Baldwin's Style: A Prospectus for the Classroom." *College Composition and Communication* 26 (March 1975), 141 - 148. Examines the use of Baldwin's style as a writing model.

FULLER, HOYT W. "Contemporary Negro Fiction." *Southwest Review* 50 (Autumn 1965), 321 - 335. Explores the "protest" categorization of literature written by black Americans.

GAYLE, ADDISON, JR. "A Defense of James Baldwin." *College Language Association Journal* 10 (1966), 201 - 8. Accuses Robert Bone of an "extrinsic" criticism of Baldwin's works.

GILES, JAMES R. "Religious Alienation and 'Homosexual Consciousness' in *City of Night* and *Go Tell It on the Mountain*." *College English* 36 (November 1974), 369 - 380. Argues that Rechy's literary contribution is more significant than Baldwin's because he emphasizes his homosexuality instead of his ethnic identity.

GROSS, BARRY. "The 'Uninhabitable Darkness' of Baldwin's *Another Country*: Image and Theme." *Negro American Literature Forum* 6 (Winter 1972), 113 - 121. Extended discussion of the color imagery.

HENTOFF, NAT. "It's Terrifying." *New York Herald Tribune Books*, June 16, 1963, sec. 6, p. 1. Discusses some of Baldwin's views on the racial climate in the early 1960s.

HOWARD, JANE. " 'Doom and Glory of Knowing Who You Are.' " *Life*, May 24, 1963, p. 86B. Includes brief comments on Baldwin's philosophy and artistry.

HOWE, IRVING. "James Baldwin: At Ease in Apocalypse." Review of *Tell Me How Long The Train's Been Gone* by James Baldwin. *Harper's*, September 1968, p. 92. Detailed commentary on Baldwin's failure to portray realistic characters.

JONES, BEAU FLY. "James Baldwin: The Struggle for Identity." *The British Journal of Sociology* 17 (June 1966), 107 - 121. Considers Baldwin's redefinition of the "black problem" as a "white problem" one of his significant achievements.

KIM, KICHUNG. "Wright, the Protest Novel, and Baldwin's Faith." *College Language Association Journal* 17 (March 1974), 387 - 396. Views the Wright-Baldwin controversy in terms of their different views of man.

KRIM, SEYMOUR. "The Troubles He's Seen." Review of *Going to Meet the Man* by James Baldwin. *Book Week*, November 7, 1965, p. 5. Argues that Baldwin's artistic appeal is due primarily to his sensitive use of language.

LEVANT, HOWARD. "Aspiraling We Should Go." *Midcontinent American Studies Journal* 4 (Fall 1963), 2 - 20. Discusses Baldwin's essays as compelling examples of the clarity and power of his prose style.

LEVIN, DAVID. "Baldwin's Autobiographical Essays: The Problem of Negro Identity." *Masschusetts Review* 5 (Winter 1964), 239 - 47. A study of Baldwin's mission in three volumes of his essays.

MAYFIELD, JULIAN. "The New Mainstream." Review of *Soul on Ice* by Eldridge Cleaver. *Nation*, May 13, 1968, p. 638. Sharply critical of Cleaver's detailed analysis of black male-white female relations.

O'DANIEL, THERMAN B. "James Baldwin: An Interpretive Study." *College Language Association Journal* 7 (September 1963), 37 - 47. Examines the factors involved in Baldwin's remarkable popularity.

SMITH, SALLY. "James Baldwin: The Expatriate Becomes Disillusioned." *Atlanta Constitution*, May 19, 1976, p. 21. Discusses Baldwin's expressed optimism that blacks will survive and triumph in America.

SPECTOR, ROBERT DONALD. "Everybody Knows His Name." Review of *Another Country* by James Baldwin. *New York Herald Tribune Book Review*, June 17, 1962, sec. 6, p. 3. Analyzes the inability of the characters to communicate with each other.

STANDLEY, FRED L. "Another Country, Another Time." *Studies in the Novel* 4 (Fall 1972), 504 - 512. Discussion of the structure, theme, and symbolism in Another Country.

_____. "James Baldwin: The Artist as Incorrigible Disturber of the Peace." *Southern Humanities Review* 4 (Winter 1970), 18 - 30. Discussion on Baldwin, Wright, and the problem of protest literature.

_____. "James Baldwin: The Crucial Situation." *South Atlantic Quarterly* 65 (Summer 1966), 371 - 81. Discusses Baldwin's conception of a "good writer."

STRONG, AUGUSTA. "Notes on James Baldwin." *Freedomways* 2 (Spring 1962), 167 - 71. Views Baldwin as artist, rather than spokesman.

VOLLMERHAUSEN, JOSEPH W. "Alienation in the Light of Horney's Theory of Neurosis." *The American Journal of Psychoanalysis* 21 (1961), 144 - 51. Support for Karen Horney's theory that alienation and neurosis result from the feeling that one has no active role in determining the direction of his own life.

WARD, DOUGLAS TURNER. "American Theatre: For Whites Only?" *New York Times*, August 14, 1966, sec. 2, p. D-1. Calls for the immediate formation of a permanent black theater which is neither segregated nor separatist.

_____. "The Goal is Autonomy." *New York Times*, February 2, 1969, sec. 2, p. D-9. Discusses the crucial issues facing black artists.

WATSON, EDWARD A. "The Novels and Essays of James Baldwin: Case-Book of a 'Lover's War' with the United States." *Queen's Quarterly* 72

(Summer 1965), 385 - 402. Examines the myth that Baldwin's writings have more sociological value than literary significance.

WEBSTER, HARVEY CURTIS. "Community of Pride." Review of *Go Tell It on the Mountain* by James Baldwin. *Saturday Review*, May 16, 1953, p. 14. Praises Baldwin for his masterful use of the flashback.

WILLIAMS, JOHN A. "Problems of the Negro Writer: The Literary Ghetto." *Saturday Review*, April 20, 1963, p. 21. Criticizes the tendency by white editors and critics to limit black artistry.

WRIGHT, RICHARD. "How Bigger Was Born." *Saturday Review*, June 1, 1940, p. 18. Detailed recollections of how the character of Bigger Thomas was created.

# Index

(The works of Baldwin are listed under his name)